Human

We aren't there yet

What is it that makes life worthwhile?
What ends the misery?
What makes us human?

When we answer those questions, we are on the doorstep to our humanity.

Whickwithy

Human

Published by Whickwithy
whickwithy@gmail.com

ISBN: 978-1-7348221-9-9

Human
   by Whickwithy

Previous efforts:
Sentience
A Sentient Perspective
Beauty & Fiction
Millennium
Book 6
The Sentient Struggle For Transformation
This And That
The Bane of Mankind
Ten
The History That Counts

"When will our consciences grow so tender that we will act to prevent human misery rather than avenge it?"
   - Eleanor Roosevelt

Answer: when we become human.

Our animal legacy still consumes us.

"The smell of a world that is burned"
   - Jimi Hendrix

"Power at its most vicious is a riposte to powerlessness."
   - Simone de Beauvoir

"When will our consciences grow so tender that we will act to prevent human misery rather than avenge it?"
   - Eleanor Roosevelt

"The unexamined life is not worth living"
"Let he that would move the world first move himself"
"From the deepest desires often come the deadliest hate"
   - Socrates

"History is a pack of lies about events that never happened told by people who weren't there."
   - George Santayana

"The reason why the world lacks unity, and lies broken and in heaps, is, because man is disunited with himself."
   -Ralph Waldo Emerson

"What lies behind you and what lies in front of you, pales in comparison to what lies inside of you."
   -Ralph Waldo Emerson

"A little learning is a dangerous thing
Drink deep, or taste not the Pierian Spring"
   -Alexander Pope

"We accept the love we think we deserve."
— Stephen Chbosky
         (You will see how this applies)

"I saw ten thousand talkers whose tongues were all broken"
   -Bob Dylan

   The Japanese have a saying, "One who asks a question feels like a fool for a moment. One who refuses to ask a question is a fool for a lifetime." Humanity has avoided asking a few all-important questions for all the long millennia of its existence.

We re not human yet.

Humanity remains a dilettante at sentience, a poser. We're on the threshold of something more, something human.

It is not a matter of you or me being human, sane, emotionally stable, rational beings. We're all in this together. Humanity, the human race, must become whole.

Unlike others that have found the human condition intolerable, I realized the problem is not me. It is our prehuman state.

Our sentience has been hobbled for three millennia for the most ridiculous reason. We remain in a stupour regarding our existence for no good reason.

Humanity will be human when it realizes that its family is humanity, not just blood relatives. Nothing less will do.

Humanity becomes human when it learns to love.

Scifi authors predict the future based on the immediate past. I looked a lot further back in order to unravel the present. The subject matter is complicated, but necessary for us to attain our sentience.

Table of contents

Sharing

A sentient race, like humanity, is all about sharing. It's what we do. We share thoughts, feeling, and information like no other creatures on Earth. We share new conclusions with each other.

Humanity has the unique ability to share its consciousness. We communicate with each other in a sophisticated manner. In so doing, we share our lives, experiences, and learnings to a degree never available before humanity existed. We share *almost* everything. We love to share. And, yet...

Sharing our thoughts and feelings is part of being human. It is the foundation on which a sentient race fulfills its advanced state of existence. Yet, there is a blindspot we purposely avoid.

Men have an aversion to sharing their consciousness. It is often suggested that it is genetic. It is not. It is only a quirk of history. The quirk is renewed with each generation through a complicated, confusing initiation.

Being human and sentient is far more than the gifts that Nature gave us. It is the use of those gifts in a sentient manner that fulfills the sentient state. We are not yet using Nature's gifts. The blindspot impedes the use of those gifts and our ability to share to the fullest extent.

Once we share fully, once the blindspot is removed, we become a human, sentient, emotionally stable, rational race.

Self-respect gets trampled by our inability to share all of the discoveries that are part of our unique sentient state. One particular aspect of our sentient awareness remains unnoticed. It is a crucial aspect of our sentient state that has been trampled by the animal's misunderstanding and misinterpretation.

The blindspot is a vast abyss of confusion from which we turn away. Even in our most personal space, we only consider it glancingly with the utmost uncertainty. Just do it.

Why we avoid it is a quandary indeed. We never understood its true sentient significance nor the necessity of its transformation into a human form. While sensing it, we avoid contemplating its significance.

Humanity is aware of far more than any animal. When that awareness confronted a new realization in the tracks of a very old trait, we became inarticulate and never recovered fully.

Humanity has never been sure of itself, its sentient state.

The advanced forms of sharing that a sentient race has available are many. They make us human. Communications is only one of those forms of sharing.

The potential to share and care at a level that we vaguely sense far exceeds that of an animal and our current realization.

We call that potential love. We have accepted a paltry excuse for love. The vast array of human, sentient love and its ultimate source remains hidden behind the blindspot.

Humanity has yet to gain respect for itself. We have always doubted our potential. The blindspot is an aspect of our sentient state that is completely new and, yet, we make the mistake of thinking it is almost as old as life. We have never taken it into consideration due to historical forces. We have accepted the animal's interpretation to our lasting regret.

Love begins with loving oneself. It becomes complete and fulfilled in the love of another. Love does not validate itself in another. It is fulfilled in another. It flourishes in another. It resides in the self. When self-respect is whittled away, so is our humanity and our ability to love.

The differences in orientation between animal and human are far more significant than we ever imagined. We have to wipe the slate clean of the misdirection provided by our animal legacy in order to embrace our humanity.

Only on that basis can the human, advanced form of caring become the powerful, transforming aspect of sentience in which all of Nature's gifts are utilized fully. The sharing can only then proceed to that which a sentient race requires. The fulfillment of love in every form.

When the love of the human race by the human race is fulfilled, we have succeeded as a sentient race.

Love cannot be fulfilled without the certainty that it can be shared with another. As long as the ability to share the physical expression of love with another is uncertain, we remain less than human. Sharing at that level is something only a sentient being can do. Women do it naturally. Men have struggled.

Make no mistake. It is not beyond men's capability. It is only beyond our predecessors ability to peer through the fog.

The ability to express one's love for another is compromised in men due to historical forces. Men's self-love becomes compromised over a lifetime due to these same forces.

Since time immemorial, since the first sentient thought, men have not been able to look themselves in the eye and love what they see. It need not remain that way. It is nothing but a legacy left behind by the animal from which we evolved. We have not awoken fully into our sentience until men realize they are selling themselves short. There is something more asked of them that they can deliver.

For women, the translation to a sentient state was direct. There was nothing impeding their transition. Women match Nature's requirements perfectly without any change. They give.

The male gender has had hurdles obstructing its way. Those obstacles suit the animal but not the human being. They must be overcome in order for humanity to attain an unobstructed sentient perspective.

It is easily done, once the misdirection provided by our animal predecessors is laid to rest. The animal's instincts overrode the male's full sentient potential for millennia.

This remarkable transformation of a trait of the animal into its human, loving form frees a sentient race to share its consciousness without confusion, delusions or restraint.

Men have hesitated to transform coitus into a loving event due to misinterpreted obstacles and bizarre circumstances. It is a human necessity for men to realize that they can easily transform coitus into the most natural physical expression of love.

Men's ability to share remains compromised. Men have never shared their unguarded sentience. Women give, men take, and it all starts in bed. It must not remain that way. The caricature of 'manliness' or humbled acceptance of failure to transform coitus into a loving event has nothing to do with being human or sentient. It is the not more than legacy of the animal that has been accepted without conscious thought.

Conscious thought has been suppressed since the beginning because of this conundrum.

Men have never full appreciated the scope of sentient existence and potential until now. Men's expressions of love and affection have been constrained by the unnecessary limitations forced upon sex by the necessities required by the animal. For humans, it must become the physical expression of love through sharing of the most momentous gift Nature provided for life.

Men convinced themselves, long ago, that they are unable to provide loving coitus. They are wrong. They made some poor assumptions along the way that inhibited their success.

Men have to learn to share, love, and care. It is all tied up in the male gender's success at the act of loving coitus.

Men's ability to express their love in the most intimate physical manner is built in for human, sentient males and, at some level, the male gender knows it. Their awareness tears them apart as long as it remains absent.

Men's loving ability was initially debilitated by our ancient ancestors' (dumber than a rock) inability to succeed at transforming coitus into a loving event.

As time progressed, their success became inhibited by fear of failure, wrong assumptions about what limits their success, suppression of the subject of sex, and misleading assumptions which led the stupour in which we exist.

Nature provided everything required for a man to make loving coitus (see Details). No need for pills, alternatives, appliances, acrobatics, or excuses. It is all built in. It begins with thinking and ends with mastery of one's own body. We have just never taken the prospect seriously or pondered the disastrous ramifications of its absence from the lives of fully aware beings.

We know we should be able to love and have been running from it since the very beginning.

The underlying problem has been transforming coitus into a loving event that a human, sentient, emotionally balanced race expects. We became trapped in the most bizarre misdirection that ever existed. It is truly a test of our sentience to overcome this limitation. It is the test of our sentient state. This one misdirection led to all of the others.

The consciously aware thought, which all of humanity has been desperate *not to share*, is that coitus is not yet human. That blindspot has suppressed our humanity for millennia.

The suppressed awareness occurred long ago, making it impossible for humanity to share its consciousness fully. Or, its love entirely. It has misled humanity in everything we do.

Loving and coitus are crucial components of our sentient state. They are tied together. We have been cut off from the most glorious consummation that a human can attain. It may not be for all, but our sentience demands that we transform coitus into a *loving, sharing* act. Not just a sideshow. It is no surprise that its lack has shattered our sentience and sentient state.

A human being desires to please themselves _and_ please their mate during coitus. It is a sentient expectation. We are not sentient until the expectation is met. We *know* how it should be. Men, due to misdirection, confusion, delusion, and distraction only please themselves. It is clear in everything they do.

Men desire to share that physical pleasure. It is foolish to believe otherwise. They have been hampered by circumstances.

At some level, we know it is possible. That is because we are consciously aware. Even though the subject of sex is taboo, our awareness of the situation *still* makes it a shared disappointment, not to mention the biggest disruption. It remains a failure and, yet, we know better. It should not be. That confounds us.

The most necessary transition (loving coitus) into our sentient state proved difficult for our simple-minded ancestors to overcome. Since then, the failure to transform coitus into a loving, human, sentient event has become accepted as if it were written in stone. It is not and everyone suffers in its absence. It is a blindspot in our sentient state. A human, sentient race can easily make coitus a loving event.

It is not difficult for the advanced minds of modern men to succeed. All that holds us back, any longer, is the fear of failure and the taboo regarding thinking or discussing coitus openly. We have been trained for millennia to avoid the issue entirely by our dumbstruck ancient ancestors.

The conundrum is confounding. Just as a man achieves his own pleasure, it hits him that he is not pleasing his lover. It confounds at a subconscious level because it coincides in the man with the most overwhelming pleasure known. The mind-blowing pleasure of coitus is invaded by the feeling of failure. The two events coincide causing a confused state that has held us in thrall for millennia. The failure comes at the worst time.

Coherent thought is almost entirely absent and the thought of failure remains absent. Coherency is lost.

The best most anyone has been able to do, up until this point, is find some alternative that provides similar pleasure for both. Coitus needs to be one of those alternatives.

The easy excuse has been that men can't improve the act. No one has even been willing to ask the question openly, "Can all men last longer? Can all men last as long as *she* desires?" because we are so afraid the answer will be no. Wrong. They can. Easily. Of course. We became a race of sentient beings without hope because of the unnecessary failure.

Shared consciousness is fulfilled at the most fundamental level when the physical relationship between two people is fulfilled. The fullest, loving representation of sharing begins within the confines of a relationship that extends to the physical. It is confounded when the physical sharing of the most transcendent experience of human existence is not shared fully. It also confounds when the most exquisite expression of physical love is found wanting.

In today's situation, there is absolutely no difference between a heterosexual and homosexual relationship when it comes to expressing the physical side of love, except that it is fulfilled more often in the homosexual relationship.

Shared consciousness and sentience can only become fulfilled when coitus becomes be a loving, mutually fulfilling event. Humanity's sentient state does not makes sense until it is true.

Our sentience is hampered by the hesitancy of the male gender to share its consciousness. Every aspect of a man's sharing, caring, emotionally balanced, sentient, human reality becomes constrained, filled with subterfuge.

Our acceptance of the failure of loving coitus disturbs the emotional makeup of a highly complex race such as humanity. The male gender (not a few individual men) needs to realize it can succeed at loving coitus. The human race needs to realize that loving coitus is possible and a crucial aspect of its humanity.

We have avoided these conclusions in spectacular fashion. We have avoided our sentient state. We do not yet know what sentience looks like.

If it were impossible for men to succeed easily and completely at loving coitus, it would still be crucial for humanity to at least make certain it is true and accept the fact openly. It is not.

Instead, we run from the situation, never facing it, which should tell you just how important it is that we open up.

We are human. We are not just some animal The defeated stance humanity has taken since the thought of loving coitus first crossed our minds is that we are no better than an animal. The animal's preconceptions regarding coitus have remained the rule. Those preconceptions are not true for a human.

Throughout our history, man has obstructed itself from exploring the topic with a will due to the inertia of past failure. We created a blind spot in our sentience. Mind-boggling irony.

Sexually, the woman consistently pleases her mate. The man consistently pleases himself. That is destructive to the conscious awareness of a race that shares its thoughts.

The sharing remains broken. Our sentience remains broken. *For no good reason!*

The animal's will is described perfectly by many religions, "sex is only good for making babies." Forget everything else.

The sentient mind rebels at the thought that coital pleasure is not shared equally. The transition from the animal state, that did not have enough wit to care, has been painful. It is natural for sentient beings to expect to fulfill the desire to love each other physically. It's where the love begins. It flourishes in coitus.

The man's self-respect and confidence in himself remains compromised. It has been replaced with bluster.

The complete fulfillment of love as a part of human life became a hopeless, unrealizable dream for both genders. Men are left with a vague sense of fallibility as his body betrays him. He learns how to take. His giving is compromised. The woman remains baffled. The sentient state is utterly defeated. Humanity's dreams of something more are put on indefinite hold.

The sentient mind *knows* it should be possible and *it is*. *With ease*. We are sentient. We think. We can be masters of our own bodies. We can overcome the animal's instincts with ease. Our distant past taught us defeat and avoidance of the issue. The Details chapter shows how easy can be. Once we get over our delusions and fear.

Modern man does not even consider that it can overcome the instincts of an animal and learn to love. That is all that stands in the way of our sentience. An animal's instincts say, "just do it." The ease will grow as a few men realize their full potential and put away their fears. *Loving is the human, sentient state.*

Fulfilling the ability to *make* love is more important than walking on two legs or talking in our quest to be human. It releases our ability to love and become human.

All attempts by the male to become human, emotionally stable, and loving ends shortly after puberty, as he convinces himself that he cannot *make* love.

The basis for fulfillment of a loving race begins with the loving between man and woman. It is essential to the fulfillment of a sentient race that shares its consciousness.

Loving is cut off at the knees as the act of coitus falls short. Which is about 90% (maybe as high as 99%) of the time.

The difficulty of a man learning to make love is on a similar order of complexity as walking or talking. It is just that men were taught defeat long ago. After more than three millennia of failure to overcome, we learned to accept what is unacceptable as if it were inevitable. It is only inevitable for an animal.

Early human males did not have the wits to succeed. They did, however, have the will to suppress the situation to our ongoing misery and despair that blunted and stifled humanity.

The two desires for coitus seldom converge in a single human. One gender learns to love. The other learns nothing. This disturbs the mental makeup of both genders and a sentient race. The balance between the genders is upset as sharing is obstructed. One gender is suppressed. The other goes mad.

The animal instincts intervened long ago and convinced the human, sentient male that it can't be done. The human race accepted the judgement as final. The animal instincts are more subtle than we ever expected. The physiology involved was difficult to discern. Simple to overcome.

The ongoing hopelessness is only due to inertia. There is no reason for it to continue. (see Details) The worst effect is the alienation of the two genders.

Men's failure to express love in its physical form inhibits their ability to express love and affection in any form. Can you begin to see the much larger ramifications? I doubt it.

Men's ability to love remains suppressed. It is not absent. It just remained suppressed - for three millennia. The ramifications of that have been felt far and wide. It has made a caricature of the male amidst a defeated ego. The male gender is just as lovingly inclined as the female gender, in its own way. It's just that the male's potential for love is clipped short after puberty.

Worse yet, because it has always been that way (because animals have been failing for millions of years before that and it was too difficult for our early ancestors to unravel), we have learned to justify and rationalize the failure rather than confront it and overcome it. That is disaster squared. It is insanity.

Because it is unspoken, it continues to grind away at our humanity while remaining only a ghost of a mirage. The good will between the two genders has been sacrificed all along. Insanity cubed.

Men's inability to express their love for three millennia, during which time the presence of mind of a sentient creature has been fully available, has turned our sentient existence inside out. It has caused all of the upheaval of our mad pre-sentient existence.

Our state of mind remains an animal's interpretation of a sentient existence. We are more than an animal in ways we have yet to recognize. We mimic what we know our sentience represents. It becomes a caricature. We are not human yet. We only act out the part and perform it poorly.

Of the two desires for coitus, the desire to please one's mate is paramount. It is crucial to a sane state of mind for a sentient being. The failure to do so inhibits the sentient state of mind. The alternatives are fine but they are only alternatives. They should not be required as a substitute for failed coitus. There are plenty of other reasons the alternatives might make sense.

The desire to please oneself while failing to please one's mate is destructive to the human state of being. It trains a gender to only take. It crushes the expansive love of a sentient race under its boot. It makes coitus a selfish act for the one that gains pleasure but fails to provide the same. It baffles both genders.

Because the condition is rampant, we have never evolved into our sentient state. The result has been a stupour that permeates every aspect of our existence. It damages everything.

We have been dodging our humanity and so many questions for so long, our sentient state has become a blur. Misdirection has been the order of the day for millennia. We remain in the no-man's land between the animal and the sentient state.

The animal's act of coitus is so limited that it could never work well for a sentient race. It has been grinding away at our humanity since our first sentient thought. We cannot achieve our fulfilled state of sentient sharing until coitus becomes a loving act of sharing the most resplendent pleasure of our existence. The failed attempt to make the most crucial sexual act (i.e. that which creates life) a loving act has driven humanity mad for three millennia. We remain an animal attempting to cope with a crucial sentient issue. Making it worse has been our inability to confront the situation. We hid, like a baffled and pouting child.

Sentience is about the advanced form of caring that we call love that includes sharing at a level never experienced before humanity and seldom experienced since. It is sharing that begins in the physical realm and extends into every aspect of a sentient existence. It is a sharing that is only available to a sentient race. Alternatives for loving will continue but they must be *alternatives* for loving.

Any man can learn to express their physical love during coitus. (see Details) You're welcome. Every man, by that I mean the entirety of male gender, needs to learn that it can express its love in its most natural physical form. It needs to become part of the human shared consciousness. It frees the conscious awareness of a sentient being to be fully shared. It liberates the conscious awareness of a sentient race. It needs to be firmly established that the male human can *easily* learn to love.

We have avoided the possibility for so long by substituting nonsense, deceit, delusion, distraction and destruction for love. The attitudes of fear of failure and suppression impede.

The chapter on Details explains what the male gender must learn. The rest of this book attempts to explain why. It is only a beginning, but Details clearly shows how easy it can be for a thinking male to learn to love with a will and become human.

While it may not be entirely clear to you, thinking and will are inherent human characteristics.

They have been relegated to a stupour.

The biggest obstacle is the brainwashing that has convinced most every man to avoid the issue at all cost for fear that he cannot succeed and his sanity is a risk. Note that there is little sane about the male gender or the prehuman condition, at this point in time. As it becomes commonly accepted, the act of loving coitus will get even easier as we put away the fear and embrace love, one's mate, and our sentience.

Can you see how the failure drives us mad? How the human, sentient state of mind becomes fractured in an awful manner?

Men take, women give, and it begins in bed. Since I fear that you will skim over the previous sentence, I ask you to pause and think that sentence through. It need not remain that way.

The male gender's state of mind is filled with the shameful feeling of failure. If that were not true, why is it that the topic of coitus has remained unmentionable for a race that has been dominated by the male gender that wants sex regularly? While the topic of sex has *finally* become rather open, coitus is still off limits for open discussion. If we were really okay, we would not hide the topic in shame. We would not have the desire to turn out the lights during coitus or hide under the covers.

It it were not true, why in the world would men suppress women? Misogyny makes no sense otherwise. Men have dominated women to no apparent advantage. All it has done is build a wall between the two genders that continues to grow. Why in the world would the gender that so desires sex put the opposite gender into a frame of mind in which they are less willing? Unless, men already realize they are lacking.

Misogyny is only be a subconscious compulsion for many, which makes it even less practicable. It is caused by a gender that has lost its self-respect and desires to drag down the other gender to the same level due to the all-encompassing stupour.

Men have become convinced they are not lovers. Their loving nature remains buried deeply beneath feelings of failure, brainwashing from an early age, intractability, stupour, and the failure itself that has absolutely no reason to continue to exist.

Men can love.

If coitus were a loving success in a male dominated race, it would not be hidden in shame. More so, it would not be a male dominated race. It would be a race of human beings that can fully *share* their experience, existence, and the celebration of the loving act of coitus. Equality and equitability of women can become the norm without legislation or bitter feelings.

The first thing we must do in order to be a sentient, human, emotionally balanced, rational race is be honest with ourselves. We are so far from that, right now, it is staggering. It becomes more convoluted every day as we justify our sentient failure.

We should be doing everything well. But, just like coitus, we make excuses and accept the miserable with lethargy. We are confounded. We remain a race caught in the trap of an animal.

We must become human, sentient, and loving in every respect.

All of the grubbing aspects of our current existence are the detritus left over from evolving from an animal. We have never crossed the threshold into our sentient state.

Loving coitus is integral to the sentient state and sanity of humanity. Our sentience is here to stay. It is just matter of whether we embrace it or not, whether sentience drives us insane or not. Coitus may not be the only form of sex desired, but the availability of the most natural, essential form of sex as a loving act that creates life is essential to our sentient state. Without it, we remain an animal in a stupour. Loving coitus is not even difficult. The stupour is difficult.

We can be an emotionally stable, rational, loving, equal race of sentient beings by learning to love in its physical sense. Without it, we remain an animal. Men need only get over their fear of failure and succeed at loving in its most natural form.

It is easy to lose one's self-respect and sentient way within the madcap existence of the prehuman. It will be nearly impossible to lose our sentient essence and self-respect when it is not undermined before we get our bearings. We will not lose our humanity when we do not convince ourselves of foolishness.

Rite of passage

It's not like an education, as such.   It is like opening the floodgates to our sentient state of mind.   You don't teach a man that he can love.   A man will know.   You have to teach the animal that it can actually be a man and can make love during coitus.   *Making* love is initiated by *sharing* the pleasure.

A man need not follow the instincts that makes the animal's form of coitus an unacceptable debacle to a human (see Details).   Going beyond the bounds of rutting coitus makes us sentient.

The misdirection that has led humanity astray for three millennia has deepened into a smear campaign against sentience, humanity, and love.   It is wrought by the animal's mad attempt to survive in a human form amidst a sentient existence.

The male gender is left with a feeling of insecurity as long as they cannot love women the way that they deserve.   All men are compensating in one way or another.   Do not blame men.   Blame the inertia of a developing sentient race that hasn't faced a sentient reality.   We will love or die.

We have never understood what it means to be human and sentient.   We have taken the easy route of remaining an animal with too much brainpower.   That has caused a disaster for three millennia.   Being human means far more than we realize.

Unraveling the mess has been a lifetime effort.

Humanity has unacceptably limited itself to an animal's existence.   The sentient horizon has been too distant, too indistinct for the animal to perceive.   We are no longer an animal in any way - except one.   It is time for that limitation to end.

Men have allowed themselves to be ruled by the instincts of an animal.   That has clipped their wings and we remain an animal.   Overcome the instincts of an animal and a man can love instead of justifying his inability to love in so many ways.

Nature provided all of the tools for humanity to become sentient and loving; from the desire for clarity, to the intellect and awareness to assess existence in far greater detail than that with which a simple animal can cope, to the curiosity and imagination to realize that we can be so much more and how to get there.   We only stumbled badly for about three millennia as we first gained serious cognition.   It is time to recover.

Maybe most amazing of all is that Nature provided all of the requirements to transform the animal's rutting enactment of coitus into a human, loving act that creates love by sharing *equally* in the pleasure of the moment. You want to talk equality? This is where it begins and it will not exist elsewise.

The transcendent moment must be shared in order for humanity to fulfill its loving, sentient state of mind and rid itself of the confusion caused by the failure during the momentous act.

Humanity has waited three thousand years to finally shake our heads in wonder and realize we are so much more.

You cannot truly believe that the human race, not this or that individual, cannot succeed at making coitus a consistently loving event. Our wits and Nature's gifts are perfect for the job.

We *must* become fully sentient. There is no middle ground. We *must* cross the threshold. We must succeed at the rite of passage that Nature provided. It has always been up to us.

Men in most cultures have created a pitiful rite of passage into their manhood. As with all else, it only mimics our human desires. This is the real rite of passage that we always knew should occur. It is the rite that counts: men become human by learning to love in the most natural physical manner possible. It is more than a rite of passage into manhood. It is the rite of passage into men's humanity. It is up to men to take the lead in fulfilling our sentience, as they have been attempting to do all along. The rite of passage is before you. (see Details)

Women have led the way into our sentience, so far. The female gender is stunning. It is time that is recognized.

Clarity

Sentience is all about seeking clarity. 'Perception is reality' is a foolish term of the animal attempting to cope with a sentient reality that is far beyond its capabilities. Humanity has a depth of perspective on existence that so far exceeds the animal that it created something new.

There is a desire for clarity due to our overwhelming conscious awareness of reality and the ability (that has been compromised until now) to discriminate the truth. Combined with curiosity, our desire for clarity becomes a requirement for sentient behaviour. Without it, we remain an animal demented by the gifts Nature granted that humanity never fulfilled and became undermined by false perceptions. We have lied since the beginning for one simple reason. We couldn't face what seemed to be the truth but was the worst lie ever.

It started with humanity turning a blind eye on the rutting act of coitus because our witless ancestors could not determine how to succeed at loving coitus which, in turn, has caused us to turn a blind eye on humanity and our sentient state itself. It is the inertia of the animal and its instincts, nothing more. We remain caught in the trap of the animal.

We have the ability to discern so much more than any animal. Not just the tree in front of you, like an animal would, or the stars, or quantum entanglement with which we have become so enamoured; but the crucial nuances of a sentient existence, like love and noble characteristics, that didn't matter before humanity. Animals make no determination. We do. We need to turn our eye and look in the mirror to see our humanity, our sentience.

We perceive the nuances, yet we still bash our way through life. We could not initially cope with a single nuance: the physical manifestation of love. Instead, we obscured and blocked a sentient reality, because we knew of no way to fulfill humanity's dream of a loving and honourable existence.

We completely denied the fact that the animal's rutting act of coitus is incomplete. We can't really avoid realizing it, though we tried desperately to do so because we thought it was beyond our capabilities. In order to avoid it, we buried it and our sentience. But, clarity cannot be avoided or denied, like it or not.

When we avoid the clarity that we know is true, we remain a demented animal, generation by generation. It enables and justifies the stupour. All that needs be done is realize it is *not* beyond our scope. We need to resolve the issue, once and for all. I have. You are welcome.

We remain ashamed of the most incredible act of existence that only a sentient race can comprehend. The act is repeated throughout a lifetime with a burden of shame. Everything regarding sex has become twisted because we have not removed the blinders from our sentience. We remain an animal seeking our sentience.

It has been a misconception, wrapped in a lie, and carried along on the inertia of paradigms of nonsense and absurdity, courtesy of the confounded animal that we remain. It was further laced with superstition, fear, excuses, and lies provided by our sentient imagination and awareness. This has caused unending confusion and utter bewilderment.

We cannot become human until the fundamental clarity of our sentient state of mind is unleashed; until we admit what is right in front of us. We can love. We can fulfill the act of love.

We don't have a chance at achieving clarity until we admit that we have barred it for millennia, especially when it comes to sex and loving coitus. We have bamboozled ourselves.

The colossal failure of our sentient state is inextricably linked to the colossal failure of loving coitus. We remain no more than an animal with our whole perspective on life forced into a deranged and miserable version of an animal's existence.

Root cause

We have never looked for the root cause of our demented state because it has been entirely blocked off from consideration.

Prehumanity has attempted to address the symptoms, never the cause, of our demented state. We legislate our humanity instead of fulfilling it. We create unending rules about human behaviour rather than learning to be human from the ground up.

I have tried for more than a decade to explain it in the fewest words possible. 'Men take, women give, and it begins in bed' is the best explanation, so far. While it states it very clearly, I'm not sure it states it clearly enough. Maybe it takes a decade and a half of studying, at this point, for that sentence to penetrate the stupour. So, I will try again to convey what is wrong.

One of the most difficult aspects of finding root cause is to look beyond the obvious. We attack the obvious aspects of our demented state with a will ... and it gets us nowhere. We attack the crazy antics, not the source of those crazy antics.

No one is even willing to admit that the largest schism is between men and women. In a few of the books, I describe it as two armed camps or the split personality of humanity. That schism is caused my women being inherently far more sentient - *at this point in time.* Men must also become sentient.

So, let's try this. Can this wrench everyone's minds free of the stupour? Men have carried a burden for millennia. They have fought to convince themselves it is okay. Women have had no say in the matter. How could they? Thus, we carried on, nose to the grindstone. Men can learn to express their love in the most fundamental manner, which is loving coitus. Humanity will remain blinded to its fulfilled state until that is so.

The natural state of a human, sentient being is loving. No human, sentient being needs to learn to love. But, the loving aspect of our sentient state can be undermined. With it, our emotional make-up becomes undermined.

It is undermined by men's inability to express their love. The love is there. Anyone that has experienced first love knows that is so. As the realization becomes clear for each man as he crosses the threshold of puberty and experiences his failure, a man begins to change, compensate for his failure in any one of a myriad number of ways. The most common is the lack of emotions or emotional control.

Undermining our loving nature becomes much more difficult, *once we attain our sentient state* as a race of beings.

Men are the ones most drastically affected in the most disturbing manner, but madness is contagious. Remember, also, women are not sexually fulfilled in the most natural manner possible. That has its own ramifications. Though not nearly as severe as the inability to express one's love and show one's affection, the inability to find someone with whom to fulfill that love has its own damaging effects. This aspect continues to grow in its preponderance in our blunted condition.

Many of the qualities that we classify as feminine are human, sentient traits that are currently missing, in great part, from the male gender. We only consider them feminine traits because they have yet to reveal themselves in men to any significant extent. Men have been limited by their inability to express their love in its most important form. The form that *makes* love.

We exist in a physical realm. Is it so difficult to understand that the physical component of love is crucial?

A man's world

Isn't it odd that, in a man's world, a world in which the male gender so desperately *requires* sexual release, the very thought of sex is suppressed *worldwide*?   Coitus, itself, has remained beyond question.   Do you even begin to understand the ramifications of that blindness, that obfuscation?   It is ongoing and grinds away more of our sentient state day by day.

All of the quirks regarding sex and the mistreatment of women across the globe are the best evidence that there is something wrong with sex for a sentient race.   Rutting coitus is the fundamental flaw in a sentient existence.   It is the one and only cause of misogyny.   Our inability to admit that there is something wrong is the strongest evidence of all that something is wrong.   We see it every day and convince ourselves that it is humanity's lot in life to be miserable.   What could be more convincing? We avoid that conclusion at every turn.

Some women seem to think that men are better off.   They are not.   The ones that wreak the most havoc on human existence hate themselves to their very core.   But, just like the failed act of loving coitus, men have learned to put on a show.   The ones that admit to themselves their failure are just miserable.   There are no good choices for anyone until loving coitus becomes accepted.

It is clear that we have purposely and forcefully avoided the subject for around three millennia.   Men forced the blindness because they could not face their failure and could not find a way to succeed.   Catch-22.   This was followed by the conditioning to never ever talk or think about sex. This made for an impenetrable guise for the failure coitus itself.   No one came close to discussing coitus because the whole topic of sex, until just lately, was off-limits.

All of this is because we were not prepared to confront the issue *and resolve it*.   Another rock and a hard place.   We could not confront the issue until it was resolved. We could not resolve the issue because we could not confront it.

That forced us into a state of stupour of untold proportions. Resolution is key.   You are very welcome.   Even though it has taken me fifteen years to explain in enough detail (I hope) to penetrate the stupour.

No options

If we ever want to become human, there are no options. Men must realize that they *can easily* fulfill the act of love in its most natural form. It isn't that men don't want to love.

Once we overcome this hurdle, *everything* changes. As we become human, fantastic horizons are opened as the stupour and seeming stupidity fade away.

Men need to know that the ability to perform loving coitus is not only possible for a man, but an essential component of his humanity. Knowledge of the ability is key. The act itself is optional. Once they know that it is not only an option but an easy one to fulfill, all of the disconcertedness that men portray, the lies, distractions, fears, and delusions of human life are gone.

After the fact, it will be clear that it is *natural* for a sentient being to love another physically. That may take a generation. The first men to attempt to love will still have to dismantle our demented state in order to succeed. It is the second wave that should begin to realize just how easy it is.

We will remain a demented animal until men realize they can make love; like no animal before. We are human. That is not just a vague offshoot of the animal. It is something completely different. Once we accept our sentient state in full the blinders will be off. Men can make love like a human, in the most natural, sentient manner possible that Nature provided for a sentient race.

Loving coitus completes the sentient state of existence.

Anything less produces only a mad animal.

Fears

There are a lot of fears that we have been fabricated to excuse the situation that devastates our humanity. All of the fears that we accept are translations of an animal's dumbfounded fears. They have no substance.

Maybe the biggest fear is fear of change in many guises. In fact, fear of change is a deeply held fear in all aspects of prehuman life.

The deepest fear, the fear that is so deeply held by the animal is the fear of affecting coitus. As if transforming coitus into a loving event could somehow upset the balance rather than correct the balance. This is, of course, the animal attempting to rescind its humanity.

The male gender, in its inability to share consciousness and love, is the standard bearer for the animal's fears. The male gender has played on these fears for millennia due to its own fear of failure. It is fear without substance, like most of the paranoiac fears that the male gender promulgates. It is a twisted view of sentient life for the gender that has not embraced its sentience.

As you go through this book, I will point out a number of the fears and misconceptions that have ruled prehumanity.

Misogyny
The riddle that must be resolved, not regulated

How in the world could misogyny make sense for any race, much less a supposedly sentient, human race?

Whenever we discuss inequality and inequitable treatment of women, it should send us right back to misogyny. It is an outgrowth of misogyny.

The riddle of misogyny cannot continue to be ignored. We dance all around it but we never have solved the puzzle of why misogyny exists. It is the only way to remove it rather than try to regulate it. It is an indication of the stupour in which we remain.

It is the most ancient riddle. Yet it has never even been questioned. Men ignore it, of course, and do their damnedest to disguise it, until it comes out, once again, in its most viral form to disrupt our existence, once again. It is the big distraction. Men are not proud of it. That's why they often try to disguise it.

Women fight it in their beautifully subtle, patient, human, sentient way, but no one asks the question. Why would any race develop such an awful trait that polarizes the two genders?

The single riddle holds all of the answers as to what is wrong with humanity.

Men have dominated throughout history. So, why would they desire to alienate the female gender? Yet, they do? It's like we are missing something. What possible excuse can be suggested, for the existence of misogyny, which can only be defined as the offensive treatment of one gender by the other? A more general definition would be that it is insane.

Men love sex. It's not in their genes, as is often suggested. It's in their balls, to be exact (and prostate, if you want to be picky). They are driven to sex by the need for sexual release.

Wouldn't it make more sense for the male gender to treat women as equals or betters, since they desire sex so much? Wouldn't kindness and unabated love of the spectacular female gender make a lot more sense?

Something is missing.

Please explain how alienation of the two genders makes the slightest sense. It is not beneficial to the race or the individual. How could men be interested in alienating the female gender?

Women are the gift and the male gender treats them like trash.

I hope you are not foolish enough to think it is not a gender-wide issue for men. It is not this or that man.

It is the whole damned gender. Some men deal with it better than others but it is pervasive and prolific.

It is buried so deeply in the male subconscious that it is passed on through generations without question or recognition.

That is a sign of just how deep our stupour is.

It kicks in at puberty and no one notices. Men's minds are filled with the nonsensical perspective regarding the two genders from the time they are born but they rail against it in their extreme youth. Until they reach puberty.

Then, it all falls in place.

Men are put in the precarious position of not being able to love the one that they so desire in the way that makes most sense for a human.

Suddenly, they become tongue-tied and unable to express themselves. Their emotions destabilize. Their humanity is ripped away from them and, though they don't even realize it, they begin to build a perverse view of existence.

At the center of it is misogyny and the precarious conundrum that exists between the genders that no one is willing to confront.

Laws, regulations, peer pressure, or other method to expose misogyny and contain it is not a solution. All of the outside forces just contain the demon ... until they don't. Like right now.

It is like clamping a lid on a cauldron and waiting for it to explode, as it always does.

Outside forces can't rid us of the bane on humanity.

I've written twelves books explaining what does rid us of misogyny and the rest of the residue left by the bane.

It's just so weird. If you were to read my books, you would find misogyny discussed in one location. The problem with laws and all of the usual 'outside forces' arrayed against the ravages of the animal are in another. I never connected the two directly.

The reason for that disconnectedness is manifold. A huge part of it is what I have been battling since the beginning. There is a disconnectedness and dysfunction that has developed regarding all things sexual. Sex is at the heart of our stupour.

There is a gaping hole in every conversation on the subject of sex. Even when we get close and brush along the outer edges of the topic of coitus. We just haven't been able to open up completely about the problem with coitus. That wrecks any conversation on the subject.

A huge part of the diffidence is the inaccurate belief that there is some difference between one man and another when it comes to coitus. The differences between men's performance during coitus is puny. It is nothing compared to what men could do if they got their head out of their asses.

No man can tolerate the idea that there is something lacking in his manhood as essential as being able to love another person. He cannot confront his suspicion that there are some men that can love, while he cannot. This explains the bravado regarding sexual exploits. While he is inadequate at the task of coitus, he can lie to himself and other men, in desperation, which distorts his thoughts further. He is no longer seeking to be human. He is seeking to be a man and he knows it's a lie.

We have never even been able to open up enough to realize that every man has the same problem and none have figured out exactly what is going on. Some men stumble upon some poor substitute, some minor improvement that they can make, like it was an Olympic event instead of an act of love. It is only an act of love when it is done right. It is seldom, if ever, done right.

The act of coitus can become an act of love for every couple.

Men believe that their poor performance is the best they can expect. They are so wrong. The male gender can learn how to love. Not just this or that individual. The whole damned gender.

Until they do, we are not human.

It is like walking on two legs or talking. A human can do it. It is no more difficult to succeed at loving coitus. Like walking on two legs or talking, it should become the expectation. It has just been incredibly more difficult to understand how a human can transform the act of coitus into an act of love.

One day, it will become the expectation. The only question is whether it is provided by the men first, or demanded by the women. The lack of that expectation is the source of misogyny. Men hide from it and women excuse it.

The successful act of loving coitus itself is simple for a human male to perform. We have just had to learned how. That is what the chapter Details is all about.

Sentience, Conscious Awareness, and the Trajectory of Life

Before the human race, evolution was exclusively a matter of genetics. With humanity, Nature introduced conscious awareness, which creates an unsurpassed way in which a sentient race can improve *itself* and its circumstances.

Thought remained a feeble representation of awareness before humanity emerged into full conscious awareness.

Attaining sentience isn't like flipping a switch. The heightened intellect and conscious awareness that comprise our sentience have been developing for hundreds of thousands of years and continue to be honed. It is a long, grueling effort.

<u>*Unconstrained*</u> conscious awareness is necessary to comprehend lofty concepts that can take us into realms unexplored. Humanity's awareness has remained fettered.

Conscious awareness allows us to question, "what is?" It also allows us to conceive of ideas that extrapolate on "what is" by asking the question, "what can be?" These concepts are further refined by asking the question, "what if?" A troubled past restrains us from applying our unfettered awareness.

Abstract ideas mean nothing on their own. Reason, with which humanity was also gifted, can and should complement the effort. Reason has also been compromised.

If, in the overall scheme of life, an idea is attractive but the results remain tentative, we retain the idea, attempt to refine it, and study its potential and its validity versus circumstances.

Concepts, like love, peace, and the nobler characteristics (e.g. honor, integrity, dignity, generosity, compassion, etc) have mostly proven unworkable. Though they hold promise, more and more they have become labeled as wishful thinking because our conscious awareness remains handicapped by our past.

As conscious awareness became increasingly capable, the circumstances humanity confronted exceeded our capacity to comprehend and adjust. Intellect was not yet capable enough to resolve the most important issue with reason.

Often irrationality has prevailed. Once accepted, irrational explanations are often extremely difficult to vanquish.

Our inability to achieve those higher ideals is due to a certain irrationality accepted long ago. "We are only human." Humanity never gained respect for itself due to a crucial aspect of sentience that remained missing. It has inhibited humanity's sentient ideals.

Our conscious awareness was duped. We became convinced that we are no more than a sophisticated and dangerous animal. We remain in a stupour of bewildering proportions.

Our conscious awareness revealed too much too soon. A key link regarding what makes us human remains missing. Our intellect could not keep up with what our conscious awareness revealed. It never recovered. It remains blinded.

Comprehension, clarification, and guidance of our own existence, due to conscious awareness and reason, are Nature's most powerful tools to lead human, sentient life into unbelievable realms of success, far exceeding genetics.

We remain stunted due to a lingering issue. Our ancestors crafted a thorough scheme of denial, resembling the River Lethe, regarding one aspect of sentient existence. When we approach the issue, our minds go blank. We avoid the issue at all costs.

We have gone down a long and weary path of developing self-defeating concepts like supernatural beliefs, existentialism, authoritarianism, always denying our own staggering potential.

An animal's reactionary viewpoint, reminiscent of a death wish, utilizes violence to achieve obscure, witless, and meaningless goals. That is defeatism, not sentience.

The break in the chain began when humanity faced an immensely perplexing situation far beyond its initial sentient comprehension *and* ability to cope and adjust.

Our early ancestors had not yet developed the powers Nature grants a sentient race in the form of reason and intellect. Instead, through imagination and creativity, they inadvertently obfuscated and blockaded the attainment of a fully functional sentient state.

The curtain of obfuscation has grown to untold proportions over the millennia. In front of the curtain, we see a demented animal. What lies behind the curtain is our humanity.

Humanity was put in the awful position of resolving a seemingly impossible issue or forcing blindness on humanity.

Resolving the issue, at the time, was just not possible. That left obfuscation on a scale that is difficult to imagine. For very important reasons, the dilemma was considered dangerous to expose, since our very existence depends on it.

Sentient awareness never rests. It is always seeking clarity. The animal that we remain had to obscure that awareness. Our conscious awareness has continually pounded against the bars erected to block clarity. Every youthful generation attempts to break through the nonsense. It took my entire lifetime to do so.

It is now in the hands of humanity to implement the resolution. This book and the previous eleven delve into the issue *and* its resolution in great depth and detail. You are welcome.

The issue was created when the first form of life engaged in the activity of creating life while only _one_ gender achieved a state of bliss that is *obtainable* by _both_ genders _of a sentient race_. This only became apparent due to the conscious awareness, intellect, and reason provided by a sentient state. We stopped halfway and cursed our sentience instead. The resolution was not simple to isolate but it is ridiculously simple to implement, once the fear is gone. Again, you are welcome.

The issue created by conscious awareness is simply stated. *For a sentient race*, there are two desires for coitus. Please oneself and please one's mate. The two desires have never converged because the full capability of a sentient race was never applied. In the current rendition, just like an animal, one gains pleasure while the other provides pleasure. That is fine for witless animals. It is not acceptable by humans of either gender. It wreaks havoc on everything regarding the sentient state.

Men take, women give, and it begins in bed. It need not remain that way. *Human* resolution is clear and straightforward.

Until that changes, we remain a demented animal out of sorts with our human potential and awareness. Our humanity requires that the animal act of rutting become the human act of loving.

The only *complete* resolution is when the *unassisted* act of creating life also becomes an act that creates love by *sharing* the incredible, transcendent gift of transcendent pleasure. The act only creates love when it is *shared*. *Both* genders suffer in its absence. The concept of love remains damaged.

Can you begin to see how this would have confounded our ancestors? They were at a loss for resolution. They handed down their bewilderment and defeat, generation by generation.

We twisted the situation and ourselves into knots because we were convinced that men could not succeed. The implication was that men were undeserving of a sentient state. We have been so very wrong. We mistakenly accepted the conclusion that we are no better than an animal at the most important act of living.

This loving act transforms humanity into a fully sentient race. It frees us from the shackles of the animal entirely.

Transforming the life-creating act of coitus is the missing piece of the puzzle to fulfill our humanity. The lack has induced the human race's emotional upheaval and, through obfuscation which resulted in a state of stupour, impeded our conscious awareness, reason, and fulfillment of our sentient state.

It crippled us. The phrase *make* **love** has meaning. Maybe *fulfilling* **love** would be more accurate but let's not quibble. Without the physical sharing of the transcendental experience *equally*, the concept of love remains barren.

Loving coitus is the crucial aspect of the Trajectory of Life in order for a sentient race to take the reins of its existence in its own hands and expand the Scope of Life.

Love and the nobler qualities are natural extensions of a fully functional sentient life. They are the first steps along the extended Trajectory of Life provided by sentience.

Our dystopia is a by-product of the stupour that is eliminated with ease by a race in command of its sentience and love.

It is not utopia. It is stable emotions, rational thought, conscious awareness, and reason transforming our higher ideals into actuality as sentience becomes a way of life. It is human.

Men were undone by the misbelief that a certain aspect of their sentient existence was beyond their measure. Make no mistake. Nature provided all required for a man to achieve loving coitus.

Noble characteristics will appear in full force once the male gender gains its sentient confidence and self-respect.

The obfuscation began due to the bewilderment of our earliest ancestors. It became a force of its own over the long millennia as it was inadvertently and subliminally embellished to counter our growing conscious awareness.   The animal remains in charge. The cowering fear that there is nothing to be done holds us back from launching into the full Trajectory of sentient life.

Transformation

If you look for the madness today, you should be able to see it. It is driven by the tentativeness and uncertainty of men. It is disguised as pompous certainty and inept execution used to mask the feelings of incompetency and insecurity. They have played a pitiful bluff on themselves in order to cover up that which *can be resolved.* That bluff has derailed the entire human race.

The fear of facing the lack continues to unmoor men.

Humanity has not allowed itself to see past the animal's circumstances to realize that a human can *think*, thereby make coitus a loving act. It is not a simple thought. It was well beyond our ancestors competency. Comprehension can only be fulfilled by confronting the fear _and_ resolving the issue. I have taken care of the latter. It is up to you to confront the fear.

Anything less drives humanity mad. That is why it took three millennia to discover it was only the instincts of an animal holding us back. The fact that the brain essentially goes haywire during coitus and orgasm has been part of the reason it has taken so long for humanity to face the issue and become human.

Our conscious and subconscious awareness became subjugated, our sentient reality deranged. That could only happen if our highly developed curiosity and intelligence were inhibited from considering the subject rationally. There were many valid reasons for the inhibition that no longer remain true.

Loving coitus is a complex thought far beyond early humanity. It is simple enough for modern men to succeed with ease. The instincts of an animal that impede the loving act can be mastered by the conscious thought of a fully developed human being.

At the time, long ago, when our conscious awareness realized the situation, humanity's insight, intellect, and knowledge were not adequately developed to address the problem. The creativity and inventiveness, though, were in fine form to obscure the issue. They obscured it so thoroughly that it has taken us three millennia to recover our senses enough to inspect the situation.

Feeling cornered, humanity cursed the realization and the very awareness that provided it. Sentience was considered a curse and a mistake, not the tremendous leap that it is. Remaining in the stupour was the only possible solution until we could develop the razor-sharp capability to confront *and* address the issue.

Coitus was too important. They could not accept that it was lacking, nor could they resolve the issue. Thus, caught in an inexorable bind, the stupour of the animal remained.

Our advanced intellect was unprepared to face such a critical issue that had existed long before humanity arrived on the scene.

The misbelief, that Nature had cursed humanity, has echoed down through the ages. Nature provided all of the necessary capabilities for a sentient race. We were not prepared.

In desperation, they blamed it on some fictitious god and/or devil. They blamed it on women. Just make it all go away. And, thus, humanity was confounded for ages.

For millennia, we looked to the skies for validation rather than relying on Nature and ourselves to provide validation.

We have always needed to validate ourselves rather than looking for some god to pat us on the head and tell us it's okay.

Coitus is not an act of love until it is *mutually* fulfilling. Nature provided for that. All we ever had to do was look.

Nature made us sentient. Women are equipped to achieve climax just as a man is. Only animals are witless enough to not realize it. It will drive a sentient *race* (*do not* think individuals, think *race*) mad as long as we continue to make excuses and not face up to the problem. There are so many facets to the problem itself, not to mention all of the problems it spawns directly and indirectly, that I have had to write twelve books in an attempt to cover as many variations as possible to dissipate the fog.

At first, when a man fails to love a woman, he may attempt to shrug it off as he has been conditioned to do since the crib. His mind will very often attempt to blank it out. That is just not possible. While, most often, it doesn't reside in the conscious mind, it will always lurk, roaming free in the subconscious. I become more and more convinced that the subconscious is a legacy of the animal that will disappear as we accept our reality.

Part of the problem is the stunning effect of orgasm. What irony! At the moment of the most transcendent experience for a man, the realization should hit that it's all been one-sided! It takes a lot for a man to face that issue, own up to it, and find some way to express his love for a woman physically. Kudos to those that do. But, as I have repeated, it is not enough. It is not about this or that man. It is about the male gender learning beyond doubt that they can succeed at loving in the most natural manner possible. It has to become part of our consciousness.

Men can love in a uniquely sentient way, during coitus. Until that potential is fulfilled, the male gender is not human. It is not that there is anything wrong with alternatives. They will almost certainly continue to be of value in the future. It is that they need to be *alternatives*. It is that coitus, the primary, most obvious choice is *not* an alternative for love-making for most men.

Every man needs to know that he can succeed at making loving coitus, even if the opportunity never presents itself or it is not a viable option for one of many reasons - as long as none of those reasons has to do with a man convincing himself that he cannot succeed at loving coitus.

We need to know, beyond a doubt, that we are human in every way. Loving coitus is a huge part of being a sentient race. The fact is that many couples would prefer loving coitus and they are denied the opportunity. Not through choice but through the male gender unnecessarily limiting itself to an animal's constraints.

Someone, during my earlier writings attempted to suggest that it doesn't matter. That the conversation had moved on. Of course it matters and it always will. Coitus is the only form of sex that is a certainty if we wish to continue to exist. Loving coitus establishes us as a fully sentient race. Without coitus, we cease to exist. Without loving coitus we will never attain our sentient state. We will continue to lie to ourselves.

When the moment comes (pun intended), many just close their eyes and shuts down the brain. That is instinctual. The instincts of an animal. Over a lifetime, it eats away at a subconscious level. The reason it stays in the subconscious and the reason it may drive a man mad is because men have been unwilling to think or talk about it. It just spins around in a vacuum in the subconscious. Why do you think that is the case?

If you look around closely today, it is clear that the most horrible renditions of humanity exist in old age. Something is lost. It is replaced with a mindless rage. That is because we have abandoned all hope of resolution. The hope remains.

Humans have been trained for millennia to avoid the subject. Why do you think that is the case? It is not because we are content with the situation. It is because we are ashamed of the failure. We've known all along that we should be able to succeed.

All men are affected in some way, to some extent. You will never hear the conversation, "Well, don't I suck at sex!" (mmm, maybe pun intended). "I wonder if anyone else does?"

Very few men succeed. This has only begun to become clear during the last century. While that may ease the paranoia of the male gender, it is not enough to make us human, sentient, loving.

We avoided the realization that any man can easily achieve loving coitus *for more than three millennia!* There is only one way that could happen. The silence is deafening. We hated the lack and were *certain* there was nothing to be done.

We substituted distractions in the form of chaos for the full panoply of love because we did not want to face the failure (think all of the awful antics of the male gender; and, yes, it has even extended to the female gender in cases; not just today but throughout history). That is not human, sentient.

It is just embarrassing once we realize *there is no reason for the failure for any man!* This defines the current destabilized state of mind of the humbled, compromised sentient being. It destabilizes our emotions, our conscious awareness, our clarity (think truth vector) and cripples our reason. It ripples outward into every aspect of life. Men can become self-confident, gain their self-respect; not just sadly attempt to disguise their failure.

We are far more than an animal. We think. In this most critical case, we have not thought at all. Sentience should not be considered cursed. It is magnificent but remains handicapped.

We outgrew our animal perspective long ago. I place it at about three thousand years ago for various reasons. Pandora's Box, Sappho, and the Kama Sutra are three of those reasons. They all occurred about three millennia ago.

Another reason I place it in 1st Millennium BCE is that coherent thought began about the same time. It began during the Ancient Greek Classical period. The corollary seems to hold true in the East, as well. In the West, it began around the time of Socrates. Pre-socratic writings that remain are mostly gibberish or simple-minded thoughts. It is offensively incoherent.

The all but silent struggle

There has been an ongoing struggle between the animal's reality and the newly minted human, sentient reality that has been attempting to establish itself for three millennia.

The human, sentient mindset has remained confounded. It has been a limited, cornered, and fearful reaction to comprehension far beyond the original bounds of an animal. All because the animal's enactment of coitus confused the issue. The animal's mentality was well established and carried forward. It is brutal.

Make no mistake, the animal cannot win. The sometimes proffered prehuman mindset of reverting to the animal is ludicrous and pitiful (think Garden of Eden). Human consciousness will not go away. We will move forward. Either in pain and misery or full accord with our sentient state.

The only possible means of obliterating the human consciousness is to obliterate humanity. We are well on our way.

If you look closely, that aim of destruction is becoming clearer and clearer as the animal flounders, caught between two worlds. The longer we remain only an animal, the worse it will get.

For awhile, we attempted to 'rise above', proceed into the human world. That effort began to fade more than two centuries ago. We are getting closer and closer to accepting humanity as a demented version of an animal. Only one failed act impeded our progress into our sentience, clarity, and humanity.

Our path remains littered with the detritus of despair as many continue to give up hope and others retain the hope but no answer. I have termed this the split personality of humanity.

It is all understandable but that does not relieve the stress that is, once again, reaching its limit. Take a close look at the leaders that are, essentially, propounding deconstructionism (fascism, by any other name) and you will see the remnants of a man attempting to prove his worth and manhood by destroying the world and obliterating the hopes and dreams (that are perceived as foolish by the animal that has only learned hate) of ever attaining our humanity. Behind it all is the frustration of men regarding the lack they have not yet conquered. In their despair and lack of resolution, they destroy.

<u>Maslow's Hierarchy of Needs</u>

Loving coitus, the missing component of our humanity, fits nicely into Maslow's Hierarchy of Needs at the Social tier. Only loving coitus leads to unquestioned self-esteem for the man. The woman's self-esteem does fine, when not dominated by a man.

The hierarchy itself suffers from prehuman conceptualization. As prehuman, closer to the dimwitted animal than a whole sentient human, we remain focused on the individual, as does the hierarchy. As a fully developed human race, we will soon accept that the pyramid cannot be fulfilled by an individual.

Humanity is stitched together at the most fundamental level by the shared consciousness of its sentient state. The shared shame and lack of love of the prehuman state debilitates.

The shared consciousness of a fully developed sentient state remediates the damage. This realization will become increasingly apparent, as we attain our confidence, not only in ourselves, but in the human race. We succeed as a sentient *race.*

Once accepted as a goal for the full achievement of our humanity, the order of the tiers not only suits but, to some extent, reinforces the reason it took three millennia.

We had to attempt to stabilize first. When all attempts at stabilization proved unworkable, it was time to look elsewhere (one may think in terms of love, peace, and the noble characteristics as a simplified description of the search for stabilization that never went beyond the surface issues; or one can think in terms of the blindness that impeded success).

The search elsewhere began, in earnest, at least two hundred years ago, though traces of it extend back at least three millennia.

Many of the characteristics of the hierarchical tier of Safety and all of the characteristics of the Social tier remain suspect or wholly undone, depending on just how sceptical you are regarding the state of the prehuman condition.

This may explain better than any other perspective how disastrous the absence of loving coitus is, as well as how important it is that the realization occurs now. All of the forces at play have been directing this effort since the very beginning. With the gaping hole in the search, we are, now, at a loss.

We cannot achieve even the third Social tier, nor fulfill the components of the second tier of Safety, until the component of loving coitus is firmly in place.

And, yet, in our lingering madness, we continue to be off and running in our attempts to reach the peak as individuals.

It can never work. That is an animal's game. We are far too sophisticated to succeed as anything less than the human *race*.

The foundation of our humanity is based on a sentient state. That means loving coitus. The necessary intent of humanity, a sentient race, is to achieve the goal of self-actualization and transcendence species-wide. Nothing less has any meaning.

It can only succeed once we rid ourselves of the disturbance (I am so dying to say, 'in the force'!) at the heart of our humanity.

In its absence and ongoing blindness to the importance of loving coitus, we continue to court disaster. It is the common denominator that fulfills our sanity and our humanity. Anything less is pipe dreams, misconstructions, delusions, and degradation of the sentient reality as it runs closer and closer to the edge.

I am now certain that self-actualization and transcendent tiers of human existence can and will occur within a few generations, once we learn to love in its full panoply of expression.

Self-actualization should be completed in three generations from the time we begin to grasp the importance of loving coitus. Transcendence should not be far beyond that.

We cannot even come close to the hierarchical level of Esteem until we learn to love. *Really* learn to love. The crucial component of loving coitus is essential and remains missing.

Madness

Imagine an instance. Let's say, that we had never figured out that we could walk on two legs. For some reason, the capability had been forced into hiding. That would be pretty horrific, right? Once we realized the possibility, we would want to remedy the situation immediately, right? We would make it clear that the human race was meant to walk on two legs.

What actually happened is much worse. We never determined how to love. That is an essential component of a sentient existence. While we have sidestepped it for ages, it is no more difficult for a man than learning to talk, walk, or ride a bike. That is what humans do. They think and they learn necessities.

We need to make it clear that to be human means to love.

We talk a lot about love. It remains a vague term as long as loving coitus is absent. We had to force-fit the word, love, to suit the situation rather than admit that something was missing.

We have been unwilling to face the conundrum that causes this inexplicable situation because our ancient ancestors were utterly confounded by it. How could our early ancestors have possibly expected to improve on something Nature provided? They were barely more than animals themselves.

Nature and our humanity

We have always missed that Nature provided the tools *and* equipment to make coitus a loving act.

Nature left it to humanity to solve the riddle of its sentience. It's almost like a test or rite of passage into sentient maturity. Nature crafted a test in order to prove a species worthy of its sentience (to itself). I don't mean to make Nature seem anthropomorphic. It is easy to do, though, as the big picture becomes clearer. The Trajectory of Life becomes increasingly intriguing with the advent of sentience and conscious awareness.

The Trajectory of Life seems certain and predetermined. All that is missing is humanity's willingness to follow the trajectory.

In my more sardonic moments, I would describe our situation as men being the butt of a cosmic joke and women as the primary victim. That's only when I begin to hyperventilate.

We have failed with flying colours until now to address the issue for such a complicated reason that it took all of eleven books to piece it together into a whole, coherent picture.

Men have unnecessarily limited themselves, since we first evolved from animals, by following the animal's mindless instincts regarding coitus. That is all that ever precluded men from making it a loving event. This also precluded humanity from fulfilling its very evident loving nature. Considering the mindless state that orgasm seems to cause, it is no surprise.

We want to love. We have just not known how to make it so.

It was not happenstance nor was it intentional, but it has obstructed our sentient state all the same. There is an unnecessary stigma attached to sex because of this failure. The taboo, the whispered thoughts, block our ascendance into a loving, emotionally stable, sane, rational sentient state.

The lack continues to pervade every aspect of our lives as we straddle the worlds of the animal and the human, sentient, emotionally stable, rational, loving human perspective.

Being human is far different from being any other animal to an extent we have not even begun to comprehend or appreciate.

We think abstractly. We consider concepts that no animal can ever entertain. Like the startling thought that coitus should be a loving event. That it *can* be such. For *humanity*.

The startling realization that doomed us, for at least three millennia, is realizing that there was far more to the act of coitus than just creating new humans. We were doomed from the start due to the difficulty and initial coverups, which have just grown proportionately to our sentient awareness of the issue. For three millennia, the common response has been to refute the realization that coitus could be so much more for a human.

Gods of delusion

Can you hear the cry down through the ages echo off Western civilization's walls, "Sex is only for making babies!", the animal cries. The West wasn't even subtle about the proclamation.

At the most fundamental level, we somehow knew for certain we should be able to make coitus a loving event. It was impeded by the repeated failure of our earliest ancestors and, yet, we *knew* we should be capable of improvement.

Just like an animal, we bowed down in submission and accepted defeat, "That's just the way it is." We have never before put ourselves in a position to ponder the pieces in order to put them all in place. The pieces have finally been put together.

Some men will freak out to think they are being asked to improve the act of coitus. These will mostly be older men that have been trained well in their failure, rationalizing and justifying all along the way.

Others will accept the challenge. These will mostly be younger men that are unestablished in their failure. It will take those with the greatest determination and self-confidence, in the first wave, to prove the case.

Before long, as more and more men accept the challenge, the fear will subside, the ease will become well established, and we will begin to become human in all its wonder as more and more men take up the challenge. The male gender will finally realize it as been misled to remit love.

It will no longer be, "we're only human". But, "Omigoodness! We're human!" will finally be stated with savour.

The realization that the act of coitus by animals was never complete shook the very foundations of our newly emerging sentient awareness. We blocked it out with gusto and force.

Think about the precarious position that men have been in, when it comes to loving a woman. Of course, they want to love! It is trained out of them in youth and the bedrock foundation laid with the first experience of failure.

The skyrocketing sales of the 'little blue pill' that is only a substitute that can never change the human state into an unfettered sentient race proves the desire. Note that the pill is popular among old *and* young. Strange, no? The pill is a manufactured substitute for attaining our humanity that does nothing to fulfill the man's self-respect or self-confidence.

One more point. Think back to that first love. How wonderful it all seemed until it all goes wrong (for both men and women). Some women may say it didn't seem such a big deal. Tell me that, again, after forty years of unfulfilling coitus and the awkward alternatives.

Most men are just as anxious as women to fulfill love the first time around, before it proves impossible for them. Then, barriers to emotions, affection, and shared confidences begin to build.

Loving coitus is wholly human and the only act of sex that cannot be replicated by any animal. No other male animal on the planet can gaze lovingly and self-confidently into the eyes of their mate while succeeding at making the experience a fully *shared* joy for both. The lack makes the men's sentience shudder and the woman's fine humanity tremble.

A crucial point that may already be bothering some needs to be addressed. Obviously, not everyone is going to have that fulfilling loving coital relationship for many reasons that have nothing to do with capability.

That is the point. There will be a rational reason for avoiding coitus, if that is the case. It won't have anything to do with capability, or the necessity of completely blinding oneself to the lack, or justifying some alternative plan.

Every human can *expect* success *if* loving circumstances permit. Every human can expect the full loving cornucopia if the opportunity presents itself. There will be no need to avoid the situation or make excuses or face the consequences of failure.

The biggest problem, today, is that *no one* expects success. *Everyone* expects failure. Not initially, maybe, which makes the situation all that much worse. It creeps up on a person as puberty and failure slowly dawns on them and drags them along unknowingly for a lifetime of confusion and irrationality.

The situation is always changing, but in my youth a man might sense something was wrong long before he reached puberty. It was emphasized by the taboo nature of sex and the unwillingness of anyone to shed any light on the subject and the freaky reactions of adults if the topic is inadvertently introduced.

It is the certainty of *expectation* of success that is all-important, as it pervades society, supports our sentient confidence, and fulfills our humanity.

No more barriers to success; no vague anticipation of failure sensed anywhere within society, no sense that something is seriously wrong. The barriers will be *gone*.

That is the difference. It assures that self-respect remains in tact for a lifetime for all, even if the loving celebration is never enacted. Just knowing it is possible for anyone is the key.

Self-respect and the desire for love

Don't get me wrong, I can't image there will ever be any that are content with the situation unfulfilled.   It will be a disappointment, for sure.   But, not a self-respect destroying agent. The human race will flow with the radiance of humanity.

It takes circumstances in which humanity *expects* success, *and attains* it, when available, that self-respect remains unchallenged. Self-respect, today, is damaged early, repeatedly, and thoroughly. In some it fails utterly. In others, it suffers only a minor defeat. It is rare indeed that it survives in tact. Even worse, how much is all human success whittled away and distorted by the surrounding insanity?

It has gotten so bad, that I think, now, most youngsters expect failure *before* puberty. They see it coming in a big way. That continues to swing the wrecking ball through all of human life.

Think about the impact on the male mindset when he fails. The best way to ponder it is from puberty forward and, also, over the long history of our humanity. Both bring perspective.

It seems at least rare, if not unheard of, that a man reaching puberty is prepared for the utter failure of the act of coitus to meet human, sentient expectations.

It is a shock to the system that takes years, decades, or a lifetime to even begin to assimilate.

It seems highly unlikely that there are many fathers that will sit their son down and tell them to prepare for failure.

So, the poor young man (not to mention the woman) is stunned to find it is not all of which he (or she) has dreamed and been prepared to experience. They are totally blindsided with little chance to recover. Maybe true of men more than women.

Since I brought the woman in, let's look at the difference in the growing awareness of the situation.

The woman slowly realizes that she may never experience that ultimate sensual feeling (during coitus) that is common for the man, *but she never feels the devastating consequences of failing to provide that sensual transcendence by* <u>giving</u> *full pleasure.*

The man, though, does attain that feeling of devastation. What a twisted scenario! The man experiences this transcendent pleasure while not providing it. Of course, it's going to twist his mind like a pretzel! Worse yet, let me emphasize: it is while he is experiencing the most mind-blasting pleasure that life provides. What a mind-bender! It is no wonder that the brain, inadvertently, shunts the awful aspects of the situation aside. Just sleep and forget by dawn. "It was great..."

Couples slowly become aware of the situation. Their expectations are shot to pieces (even more so the closer to present time you get). Many move on to a second relationship with their expectations adjusted downward in order to cope.

Thinking it through

When you think about how it slowly sinks in to both a woman's and a man's consciousness, also think about how it has progressed over the millennia. The same complicated realization has been evolving for the two genders of the human race over a long three millennia. At first no one thought about it. Then, some few did. Then, came an uncomfortable situation as realization really set in. It was all shut down because there seemed no way out. What else could they do but hobble their conscious awareness to an extent that hobbled our humanity?

It is obviously not easy to face. We have taken three millennia to get to the point that it has finally reached the surface of our thoughts, while it is certain that the thoughts first appeared at least three millennia ago. We are still not there, but we are finally on its threshold. Its damaged trail is finally clear. I only hope I have conveyed it clearly enough.

The same holds true for the individual. It will take years for it to sink into the man's consciousness that there is not a damned chance that he will ever make it the loving event that all men desire. What a crushing defeat! Maybe true for women, also?

The man cannot even confide his 'great secret' to another. Maybe some discuss the situation with their mate. He is not about to ask another man.

Which brings up another important point. A man never learns to confide in *anyone*. All because of this failure that can never be discussed. Confidences certainly do not become a dominant trait in a man. Bluffing does. How could it when he is holding back the biggest secret he doesn't ever want to share with anyone ever? Even though, we are finally learning it is an open secret.

Which, when you think about it, is another huge mind-bender for men. He shares his 'secret', whether he likes it or not, with any woman with whom he sleeps. Pretzel squared.

To make it pretzel cubed, consider that, until just lately, no one had a clue how many men suffered from the failure (it approaches unity). Are they the only failure?!? Pretzel cubed.

I could go on. To sum it up, the delusions we have endured will make one's head reel until we open our eyes.

Everything that couples have gone through, the human race has also gone through over the millennia of our blindness. It is just a lot to take in and confront.

We have been confounded, bewildered, and deceived - by ourselves. While we shun change in general, thoughts of change regarding sex drives us to extremes. It has been becoming clearer all the time what was missing. It has not ever been clear how to rectify the situation. Instead, we made our excuses, turned out the lights, and closed our eyes and let the misery remain, distractions continue, and shame have its way.

That is another mind-boggling aspect of the situation. Look at all of the 'sex studies'. I only put it in quotes because the head spins when one takes a hard look at what is termed 'research'. (i get into this in very much more pointed detail in other books. i do not see the point in doing so, again)

It is like there are minefields around the whole subject and *no one*, even a researcher, has been willing to do more than carefully dance around the subject of coitus, always fearful of upsetting the accepted taboo status of thinking or talking about the failure *as if it were a failure.*

It's this conditioning to not ever think about the situation that clarifies just how taboo the subject has been.

It also clarifies why it has never been overturned. We never looked! The 'researchers' go off and measure this, measure that, define this, define that. Voila! Three minutes must be success! No one asks why can't it change? Why are we unbelievably stuck at a couple of minutes? Why is there a time limit?

The 'researchers' term for it is that it is all a 'mystery'.

This bring us to the situation that seemed to emerge during the 1st millennium B.C.E. There is clear evidence that we were fully aware of the lack at that time. The search was on for what to do about this onerous failure. Success took another three millennia.

Since remedying the situation was beyond their grasp, the only possible resolution, *at the time*, was to forget the question and the quandary ever existed. We proceeded to make the whole subject of sex off-limits in so many ways.

That is not easily done. It required a massive shift to make the question go away. We had to make the whole topic of sex taboo. Not just coitus. The topic of sex itself had to become verboten.

Obfuscation

This is how we derailed our sentience. We had to take such extreme measures to obliterate the question that it forced humanity into the stupour which remains to this today.

It was not enough to make the question off-limits. It was necessary to make the whole subject of sex off-limits.

The subject of coitus would never even come up for query if sex itself was taboo. One could never get close to asking a question regarding coitus. Which, by the way, you see the results of in everyday conversations today. We finally talk about sex.

We may talk about LGBTQIAWXYZ (usually in some insane confrontation), but we *never* talk about coitus. We had to make it impossible to go near the question of coitus. The triggers to avoid anything anywhere near the issue of coitus were drilled so deep that we hardly even notice them. Instead, we will argue endlessly about the right or wrong regarding all of the alternatives. Never coitus.

All of the confrontation, confusion, and disruption is due to the topic of coitus being off the table for three millennia.

But, our sentient awareness *still* keeps hammering away.

Think of the overall history as trying to erase the question by performing a lobotomy or, maybe shock therapy, which is very appropriate in many ways (think distractions and chaos). That is remarkably close to what happened, except no surgery.

We left a horrible gaping hole in our sentient state. We convinced ourselves that it was no big deal and it was best if we would just make it all go away. That was the animal talking. I still hear it today as I try to explain. The biggest disaster *ever*.

A huge part of being fully human, that can distinguish us incontrovertibly from the animal, is love. We threw it out with the trash because of a mind-bending fear of madness and failure at attempting to enact the purest form of the physical act of love. The fear was rooted in the animal and our fear for survival.

Worse yet, it essentially taught us to lie. By avoiding the question, we debilitated a vast range of inquiry, substituting non sequiturs, excuses, blind passages, and outright lies for the truth, leaving a vast abyss in our sentient awareness.

Playing dodgeball

We learned the ability to dodge questions and the truth, which we have used profusely since. By any other name, a lie. A great concern of mine is that lies are rolling off the tongue today with more ease than ever before. We live by the lie. It is all due to a dimwitted animal attempting to cope with sentient existence before it was ready to do so.

The worst part of this derailment of our sentience is that it left a stigma within the male gender's mind. Even with the massive coverup, the stigma could not be shook loose without opening our minds to the question and resolving it. It set up disaster.

All that is required is that men learn to master their own bodies. Don't go thinking it is some huge hurdle, it isn't. The only huge hurdle is getting over the ingrained fear of failure and unwillingness to look at the problem as a human would. It is almost entirely a matter of overcoming the stupour of the animal.

Once the male gender learns it can succeed, it becomes simple.

A man only need learn discipline in order to learn how to love (see Details). The only remarkable thing about it is that it has taken us more than three millennia to see through the maze and confront the puzzle in order to resolve the issue.

All it took, on my part, to define the simple adjustments required was to rid my mind of the stigma of looking at it through the lens of fear and babble that has accompanied it since we first put our foot in our mouths and never took it out.

The worst, most cockamamie, conception that is accepted without thought is that there is any time limit. There is for an animal. *We are human! We think! There . is . no . time . limit!!!*

All it takes, on the male gender's part, is a little effort, a human will, some sense, a slight bit of knowledge (which I have provided), and the willingness to overcome the fear that has held humanity back for millennia.

Beyond knowing how to master their body, the other crucial insight is how a woman's arousal operates. It is not as straightforward as a man's. But, just as with the man's own mastery, it is only a matter of knowledge. All of it has been blocked by the stigma on sex and coitus. It is all in Details.

I will add that the younger you are, the easier it will be to succeed. Youth has not already accrued a number of bad habits and rationales that are fixed in place and difficult to overcome, not to mention the willingness to do so. They have not already built a wall around the whole fiasco. If they are young enough, they are still eager for success. Just let them loose.

It is a matter of our human consciousness grasping this last piece of our sentient reality in order to clear our sentient slate of the animal, once and for all. The sentient state is not something that crumbles at the drop of a hat. That only happens when a person has learned to *act* like human, rather than enjoying the full support and internal certainty of *being* human.

I am not talking about teaching this or that man how to make coitus a loving event, though, of course, that is where it must begin. It means nothing until the *male gender* accepts it as part of their humanity. It has to become accepted gender-wide.

Making love is crucial to a man's humanity, more than walking, talking, reading, or writing.

Our sanity only begins when the human male gender realizes that, like talking and walking on two legs, loving coitus is part of being human. Unassisted. No pills, appliances, appendages, or acrobatics required. Just the most remarkable loving event ever conceived. Eye to eye. Just like walking and talking, it needs to become a fulfilled expectation that is of similar difficulty.

That step for humanity creates emotional stability through the good offices of self-respect and self-confidence that have been undermined all along. Men's emotional stability is shot to pieces as they transition through puberty, whether they are willing to admit it or not, along with their self-respect and self-confidence as a human being. This immediately puts all noble characteristics at risk. Few survive. It wears further away over a lifetime of deluding oneself further and further. Our humanity itself has been wearing away over the last three millennia.

Again, think about the common household routine. Maybe it is not true of all. It is sure true of many. The family walks around on eggshells just waiting for father's next explosion.

A man realizing that he can love his lover face to face and fulfill *her needs* as well as his own in the most natural manner possible remains human. It unleashes his potential for love as well as his humanity. It liberates the love that has been there all along, bottled up inside, twisting through his existence for a lifetime. This puts an end to the nonsense and confusion forever.

Women rightly complain that many men never show a bit of affection. What has been lost in the shuffle of attaining our sentience is why men's affections are so often deficient. It has been bottled up inside of them all along. Loving coitus unleashes the crucial characteristic of affection and makes room for all of the other noble characteristics that I have mentioned (there's a full list in quite a few of the books) by supporting a man's self-respect and confidence in himself.

This frees men up to show the affection that has felt so false to them as they fail to express that love in its most essential physical form, especially in its most natural physical form.

No man would have ever put it in those terms but that's exactly the situation. They are dumbfounded when it first hits them and many never recover. Many never even attempt to find an alternative. The shock runs deep. They may never mention it. Most may never be consciously aware of it. It just eats away at their stability their whole lives long.

The most curious aspect is the uncertainty that men carry around with them regarding whether this is the norm. Or, is it just them and some small band of men. The bends and twists that a man incurs when thinking there is something wrong with him as an individual rather than the male gender, I have not even begun to discuss and won't. The ramifications are far and wide but, like all the others, go away once men learn loving coitus.

Try talking to any man about this subject. It won't happen. You will certainly never hear two men talk about it. There are a *lot* of reasons for that and a lot of disastrous implications that men and women have endured for millennia.

It is why the unbelievably bizarre repression of sex began. It has all inadvertently obstructed and inhibited the attainment of a fully sentient, rational, emotionally stable state of sentient reality.

This draws a line in the sand between human and animal.

I dearly hope you can see the difference between this and all of the useless 'remedies' for our mad state that are propounded. This isn't some wishy-washy proclamation that "love is good" or "love is all you need" or "focus on your navel" or "We just exist and, then we die" or "Deconstruction (or existentialism) is the answer!" It is based in the obvious, even though we avoid it.

It is a hard-nosed look at the *human* dilemma, not some fanciful poppycock that has endured for millennia through navel-gazing and proclaiming peace is the answer, while nothing changes. Or accepting, in defeat, that we will never be more than a mad animal, which I find personally disgusting. Or, depend on god to have all the answers (which essentially means relying on being dead one day; *then* all your questions will be answered??!!?!). We get closer to accepting the mad animal wholly every day as we remain at a loss as to what is wrong.

Can you even see the half measures that "love (or peace) is the answer" conveys? What answer? It is grasping at straws.

This is a realistic assessment of what it will take for humanity to rid itself of the insane confusion, paranoia, delusions, and deceits that our near-animal predecessors imprinted on our brains long ago, and which we have never confronted.

The human race continues to avoid its ascendence into a state equivalent to its humanity for no other reason than an irrational and insidious fear of this particular failure. It has *never* been considered in the light of day, much less rationally discussed. It creates a pall that hangs over all of human life. It is the darkness we fear. It is the dystopia.

The obliterating suppression of the subject of coitus for three millennia is maybe the most damning evidence of its importance.

People have even begun to take sides on every other form of sex, but this one subject, coitus, has remained silent; taboo. Take a look at the gibberish on sex we have most recently begun to utter and argue. Coitus remains off the table for discussion. No mention of coitus in any of these discussions, *even though the situation itself begs for the discussion*. It is almost as if the other discussions are only there to *force discussion of coitus*.

Talk about irony. Our humanity has been stranded for three millennia because we have purposely distracted ourselves from the actual issue that discontents our existence. It is truly insane.

We attack all of the blatant, superficial surface issues on all subjects (not just sex) that lead nowhere, while more crop up daily. We pick apart the tiniest problems as if they could make the slightest difference. Until now, the best we have done, just lately, is dance around the topic of coitus with clear shame.

I am not talking about utopia. There is no promised land, just a stable, rational, sensible, sensitive, human experience and existence that will lead places that we cannot even begin to imagine today. Even our ascent into Maslow's transcendence is not utopia. But, it is human, which is so much more than we ever imagined. It is so much more than the dystopia we will easily leave behind with all of its concocted nonsense.

I am talking about ridding ourselves of the *source* of the dystopia that so many take for granted and are absolutely certain will never go away, even though they can never pin it down.

These consider it the human state for goodness sakes! That is why the awful, offensive phrase, "we are only human" exists. What it is really saying is, "we are only an animal with too much brains for our own good." *That* is what everyone believes today.

I am trying to prove to you that we are not just animals. Nature, in a way I can't begin to imagine, prepared us for this.

We are human. We have never understood the full scope of our humanity or the truly awesome potential of love. We are still thinking of love as an animal would: caring only for those closest to you. Oh no! Human love is on an entirely different scale. Full, untarnished love begins with the relationship between an intimate couple. From there, it spreads outward like a tidal wave.

Right now, we remain little more than an animal. We are not living up to our sentient, human potential. Not by a long shot.

Bluffs

Joan Didion made the insightful comment that sex is our most durable communal joke. While true, that truth makes a mockery of our humanity. It tells us we are not human yet. Note that she does *not* mention coitus by name. The animal's taboo rules.

If we only step outside of our animal background for just a moment, it is clear that sex, coitus in particular, should be the most glorious event of a lifetime. It is the event that should transform our existence into something human rather than the event done in the dark and forgotten as best we can by morning.

I tend to use the term prehuman a lot. There is a reason for that. Look around. Do you really think this is how a fully sentient, human race would act if it weren't acting like a cornered animal hiding from something? Hence, prehuman.

Nature gave us a powerful set of tools. We have yet to put them to use. We have yet to even consider them. We barely use our intellect and have certainly not even begun to use our heightened conscious awareness.

Some may hesitate at the suggestion that we have hardly begun to use our intellect. While it is starkly clear to me, I am not sure others can see it.

We have built like madmen disregarding consequences. That is not using the intellect. That is stumbling around in the dark, always causing more problems than we resolve.

We have never taken a hard look at humanity itself. Oh, yes! We dance around the subject. We blame individuals that have difficulties "adapting" to the awful environment of the prehuman. We never look around and say something is fundamentally wrong with the human race.

"That's just the way it is. Toughen up," responds the animal. We have so many catchphrases to avoid the subject of humanity's madness. "This world is crazy" rather than "Humanity is crazy".

No, we have yet to use our intellect except to avoid the most important subject by causing distractions with any other subject or outrage. We have had no desire to look in the mirror.

Men have been running a bluff on themselves, as well as the rest of humanity, since the first day that we attained our sentience and the dilemma first became apparent.

Men have something to learn regarding how to make coitus a loving act. It can also be stated as men have something to learn about making love, or, simply, men need to learn to make love.

Don't just breeze past the phrase "make love" and accept only the vague and misdirected connotations. Read it for what it says.

Loving coitus *makes* <u>love</u>. One-sided fulfillment does not. It leaves us barren as a race. Just look around.

Loving coitus is love at its finest, most intimate, personal, and human. It is the foundation of love that has been missing from our humanity since we first emerged from the animal kingdom as something more. Without the foundation of loving coitus, love exists on a foundation of sand with the sands shifting and the tide always ranging closer, as our attempts to mature fail.

Sharing that transcendent experience in any way with anyone in a loving manner is learning to love. Sharing love during coitus has been an outlier. It has hardly existed. The act that is most natural and central to our existence remains wanting. The act that creates life has seldom created love between the couple that enact it. It is the original, most important form of sex that creates life. It also needs to create love.

The phrases "Love is good!", "Love is all you need!" are just gibberish without a foundation that can stand the turmoil of existence through success of the loving physical experience that reinforces our humanity. Loving is not fulfilled by a dull-witted, stubborn will. It is created by a race that knows how to love in the most essential physical manner that keeps us from extinction.

Our existence depends on coitus. So, does our love. Coitus should not be an outcast when it comes to expressing love in its physical aspect and there is no need for it to remain that way.

I hope you will agree that wars, maintaining a nuclear arsenals, hating people for myriad frivolous and ludicrous reasons regarding differences of no import, like race, governments, borders, and varying opinions on mundane topics is not sane. It is not human. Hence, we are not yet human.

We are prehuman. An animal with too much brains for its own good. The prehuman says, "Life is pain." "We are only human." "It's not personal. It's just business." "That's just the ways it is." from their outpost as an animal.

A human will realize so much more. "We can love with a will." "Omigosh, we are human!"

To expose the problem and explain its resolution in a logical manner is my intent for this book, though I do not plan to attack all of the minutiae. I have explained the minutiae throughout the previous eleven books as best I can. I am not going to explain how all of the frivolous concerns of a frivolous race are not human. That also is in the other books. I will, though, attempt to highlight as many as possible.

I finally realized that the past eleven books were as much purging myself of the nonsense we accept in our stupour through the fury it caused me by close inspection for the first time in human history as it was learning to convey what it means to be human. The fury, the disgust, comes through clearly in the books.

I will attempt to focus on explaining how the human race becomes sane and clears the air for its humanity to reveal itself, thereby, leaving room to think rationally without emotional upheaval and the preponderance of paranoia and delusions; and finally becomes human. I am attempting to reveal our humanity.

In other words, what I have to say is big. Really, really big. I have been working to comprehend and explain it for fifteen years. I have been studying humanity for sixty years, always wondering what is wrong. Never saying a word because all of the nonsense that I heard resolved nothing and I had nothing to add to the insane arguments of no import. Any argument I could have made would have been the same. Posturing. Until now.

Maybe the most important step I took was never taking a position on nonsense. I would never allow myself to be drawn into some conversation that has a horizon of less than a century.

It was clear something big was missing. I had no idea what. Setting my horizon on greater than a century cleared out a lot of nonsense from the sieve.

I never really expected to stumble on the answer, though after sixty years of concentration on the subject (and my mouth remaining shut and mind open), it is certainly not surprising.

I could not participate in or stand the stupour that hangs over us like a dark cloud and impedes our progress into a human existence. Something was missing. How everyone else accepts the debacle of our existence remains a mystery to me.

I had to ask myself, not long ago, do I despise the human race? The immediate answer came back forcefully, "No", but I sure despise the conditions that we endure. All of the constant upheaval is acted out on the stage of the theater of the Absurd. We are beginning to pay the price for that absurdity in full.

Human

We are not human yet. It is not enough that Nature granted us heightened intellect and awareness. We have to apply it. We have to be able to use those tools that Nature provided to distinguish humanity decisively, conclusively from the animal.

It begins with loving coitus because its lack hijacked our sentience. This crucial element's absence has obscured and sullied our way forward all along. We remain an animal until we realize that loving coitus is human.

The effect of its lack is truly remarkable. The misery we endure is its hallmark. The animal assures us, "That's just the way it is," to justify its absence and our brutal circumstances.

It increasingly distorts every aspect of sentient life as the justifications for its absence are defended and rationalized against all reason, as the glaring awareness of its absence becomes increasingly evident. Whenever it seems to be at risk of exposure, the male gender becomes increasingly unruly. Their fear of exposure is all-encompassing until the fear is gone.

What makes it all that much more confusing is that it is an open secret. It is the secret that every person past puberty knows. Yet, every new generation gets blown away by it. We are so convinced, "that's just the way it is", that we have never taken the time to realize it is not the way it needs to be.

We have attempted to transmogrify from a butterfly back into a lowly caterpillar. We have convinced ourselves we don't deserve to be human. All because we never realized that fulfilling the metamorphosis into the butterfly is dependent on the initiation of love from within by fulfilling the physical aspect of love. Though it may sound corny, it's true.

How remarkable! The race has fought against itself in order to deny its worthiness to be something far more than an animal. Somehow, we became so confused that we never realized we could never get out from under the bane carried by the animal.

For most of the last three millennia, while we had the conscious awareness, we did not have the knowledge base, clarity, lines of communication, or necessary perspective to overcome what has frozen us into the demoralized state of a cornered animal. In other words, our past failure was inevitable.

It was impossible for our earliest ancestors to overcome the bane, women shrugged their shoulders and accepted it because there was no alternative, and men breathed a sigh of relief.

We accepted what never should have been accepted. It has allowed men to remain no more than an animal.

Maybe it seemed an effrontery to the animal that remains. Maybe the animal is saying, "Are you kidding me??!? For the last million years we could have been loving??!?!? We could have been so much more??!?!?" It bends the mind to attempt to comprehend all that has been holding us back. What has made us so determined to avoid our sentient state? It is because of the way that the failure came upon us and the fear that was allowed to creep into the human psyche. The fear that men could never become fully human and share the love.

It hardly dawns on anyone until it is so late in the game of the life of an individual, that it would horrify them to admit what went wrong. Again, that selfish perspective shows itself. The selfishness is not a human trait. It is a witless animal trait.

As goes the individual, so goes the race and human history.

There is a slow whittling away over a lifetime of that which makes us human. As defeat becomes complete, self-preservation requires an alternative story to justify the degraded state. It is passed on to the next generation by avoidance of facing the situation. We act like it doesn't matter. Nose to the grindstone.

While that is most apparent in those that have completely accepted the demented state of the animal, it becomes clear that everyone of us develops an alternative story to justify their late-in-life rationalizations. Any acceptance of the true state of affairs is rejected out of hand. Paradigms of nonsense win. They overwhelm the rationality of a sentient race.

As I said early in this book, sentience is not like flipping a switch. This is the last frontier of the barren landscape of the animal that has always been necessary to cross.

Through all of the hardships and distractions of the last three millennia, a small portion of our focus has remained on the crucial question, "what is wrong with this picture?" or, if you prefer, "what is missing from our humanity?" Its discovery was certain, once we had puzzled through all of the other options that led nowhere.

In other words, we needed to discern what is really going on. We needed to ascertain and fulfill our sentient reality as we realize it is infinitely different than an animal's reality. That is the essential problem we have faced all along. We have to differentiate conclusively between an animal's existence and our own. So far, we have retained the legacies of an animal while frittering away our exceptional talents of intellect and awareness. All because we could never admit to loving coitus as human.

Converging lines

As I continue to get a better scope on our 'hidden' history; as I see past all of the glamour to the substance of what has been going on since humanity first began to think coherently about three thousand years ago; it becomes clear that so many lines have been converging on this point of learning the truth about sentient existence and why we remain so unstable and irrational.

I still worry that it could take millennia more. The dumbstruck reaction I get from most makes me wonder if we are ready yet or if I could be clearer. This is my last attempt.

All of the bitterness within our past is justified. How could we not be bitter while sensing deep within us that there has been so much we have been missing? By the time most begin to get some vague sense what is going on, their life is virtually over.

How could we not be bitter regarding the most transcendent event of human existence slipping through our fingers and remaining a miserable failure? The best we could do was assemble hints pointing to the truth over our long painful history.

It's all there and it always has been. We succeed at anything we attempt and, yet, coitus remains a miserable failure because we never made the attempt. Deep in our minds, we know it. We so purged our minds of the possibility that it hampered our ability to be sentient, loving, emotionally stable and sane.

Throughout history, the two primary vectors of blind inquiry into what was missing have been love and sex. We have studied one incessantly and obsessed incessantly about the other while avoiding *any* discussions on the latter topic. Of course, the two never converged. We never put the two together. Even though the phrase "make love" has been around for centuries. There have been many more lines of inquiry, as well, I finally realized.

It is not a haphazard accident that we have finally arrived at the point of fulfilling our humanity. More exactly, it had to be the way it was. It was, sadly, inevitable that it took so long.

Most striking to me is the ongoing attempt to elevate the human race to its humanity while, simultaneously, some do their best to tear it all down. That also is not just a coincidence. I don't want to get into it but I want to hint at something. What segments do you think strove the hardest to elevate? Which continues to attempt to tear away at our existence?

I was wrongly sceptical (as I studied our situation) regarding women's attempts to train men to *act* human. While it was misguided, it was necessary and may have save our existence. It also was inevitable. While the best it could ever do was get men to *act* human, it may have been enough. What else could women do? It also seems to have freed some men to think beyond the usual bounds. Women could not comprehend what is wrong with men, much less complain about the lack.

They certainly couldn't tell a man, "Now, here is what you are doing wrong." They couldn't ever be certain that men could do better, much less suggest how a man succeeds.

Do you see how this developed? It takes brainpower to overcome the ease of failing at coitus. Women could never say that men should be able to do better, so men were willing to accept the failure, even though it has always disturbed.

Women could do nothing about the disturbing source of so much discontent directly. If men couldn't last long enough to reciprocate the love that they were given with open arms by women, what else could women do but use their incredible patience, love, and humanity to try to guide men in the right direction to *act* human and, just maybe, see around the corner?

From what I've understood, few, if any, women ever connected the cold, distant, emotionally disturbed behaviour of men with its source. The failure haunts men, whether they admit it or not.

Women must have been mystified by men's obdurate stance and seeming unwillingness to learn affection with open arms, never suspecting where the real problem existed. Sex and love were two different perspectives on the same issue that could never understand each other, especially because one gender was just not going to talk about it in any way while the specter of failure remained. What impeded men's ability to love?   Men couldn't admit the problem and women couldn't guess.

The worst, most frustrating aspect of all is that everyone was reading from the same script that had been written by near-animals before the slightest comprehension of the foreordained sentient state could make itself known. It is the insidious nature of inertia.   What and who we were goes a very long way in defining what and who we are.   We remain an animal for one reason only.

Then, there's men.   Being as that is my gender, I feel very entitled to be irritated and not hold back any punches. Yes, all along the way, there have been men that have risen up to meet the challenge of the day as best they can.   Mostly, they have been preoccupied with hiding their silly secret or, of late, justifying their failure (e.g. sex 'research').   It's embarrassing really. Men are trying to prove they are no better than an animal.

Even that makes sense, though. That is exactly how the script was written for men until they quit submitting to the animal and learn that they can succeed at love. Then, the script can change radically and men can become human.

In the quotes that I publish in almost every book on this subject, there are a lot of quotes from men. Two that zero in on the real problem best are from Emerson.   Even those are so vague, so fearful of brushing up against the actual problem it seems almost sensed by instinct.   They are more like hints to look further (e.g. Pandora's Box).   As you read the quotes, realize how they veer away from the actual problem while indicating it.

Let me see if I can summarize in very short form the long explanation (coming up soon) I have composed to explain how men learn to last long enough to express their love in its most splendid physical form of coitus, which is necessary in order to free love to extend into any and all other forms. Without it, men remain barren of love.   The whole story is in the chapter, "Details". Enough specifics are available in Details to make it possible for any man with the slightest will to do so.

No doubt there is far more to discover. We have just begun.

"Don't twerk or jerk until the lady sings" sums it all up.

I must reiterate, since the current version of humanity seems to have the attention span of a gnat: pills, appliances, appendages, or acrobatics are no substitute for a man knowing with certainty that he is human since he can now fulfill loving coitus by lasting as long as *she* desires without contraptions of any kind.   The contraptions are just signs of the animal.

The wrench in the works

If you cannot see, by now, how this all ties together with the unspoken and dreaded realization that there should be much more to coitus and that the physical manifestation of love in its most natural form is completely dependent on the man and, further, that it is easier than anyone could possibly have imagined, goodness help me.   If you cannot see that the lack destroys any chance at sentience, I have failed.

Yeah, beginning to hyperventilate, once again.   Just keep in mind, this is my twelfth book on the subject.

It is not so much that loving coitus is required as it is that there is no reason that it continues to fail, other than the brainwashing we have all endured for millennia, thus forcing us to remain no more than a demented, mad animal.   In other words, maybe cunnilingus and any other way in which two people share sexual satisfaction would be enough, *if there was a reason that coitus fails*, other than the impetus of the animal. Humans can learn to love in the most natural form available, therefore humanity must accept that loving coitus is the only form of coitus that makes sense. Anything less is an animal's rendition.

Let me reiterate.   It will help calm me down.   The natural tendency of women to be lovely creatures comes down to their ability to give in bed with ease. Men have never had that luxury.

Men can succeed but it will take an effort. It's not like there is any other good choice. It is obvious that ignoring the failure is not a reasonable choice. The brainwashing that we have endured is at the heart of the problem.   That is proven by our current horrible state; by the necessity for clarity (i.e. facing the truth); by just looking at the havoc that men have caused. Oh, there are just so many ways in which it is clear that the failure of loving coitus destroys our ability to achieve our humanity.

It is not utopia that I describe but it is no longer dystopia. It is human. Finally. Not an animal in search of its humanity. We are not a human race until we learn to love physically.

Let me try to explain the stupour. I mention it often enough but, as the books piled up, I quit doing more than referring to it.

Men have cut themselves off from any deep thoughts, any risk of self-inspection, because of the one touchy subject banging around in their subconscious that they have never ever been able to take out, confront, and examine to any extent at all.

They have brainwashed themselves and their highest priority is to brainwash women, as well. Everything else is secondary.

That caused the stupour. It invades every aspect of our lives. It also causes distraction of the highest order. When the alarm bells start going off, warning that the subject might get broached in whatever way, the worst men become dangerously insane. Some spend a lifetime in that state without pause. The game of domination is the animal's reaction to feeling exposed.

In the stupour, men flail around trying to find some way to prove themselves. The worst usually become megalomaniacal.

Remove the failed situation; then the stupour *and* dystopia are *gone*. *Then*, we can get around to making all of life human. The stupour and dystopia are, in essence, one and the same.

I hate having to go off on tangents but I've heard it too often. "I'm fine. I find other ways to satisfy a woman." Really? Then, why do so many men (old *and young!!!*) take the pill to make coitus successful. The pill is a pitiful substitute for loving coitus. It is a disgustingly manufactured manhood. That makes it far less than human. It is an animals trick to appear human. The point is that the only reason we say, "it's alright" is because we have been certain since crawling out of our caves that there is nothing to be done. What if there were?, Read Details.

We know damn well we can do better. We have been hiding from that fact in desperation. It impedes our humanity.

Or the other answer: She says, "any way you can make it work is good enough for me!" Does that make it's good enough for you? When I ask that question, I get silence.

You have no desire to make coitus a loving act through the mastery of your own body? You have no desire to look her in the eye while you each achieve that transcendent state in the most natural way imaginable?

If you knew for certain that you could master your own body and last as long as you desired, through a simple effort, you would. Right now, you are convinced it is impossible. Not so.

Forget master of the universe as long as you are not master of your own body. More exactly, that benighted pompous desire to be master of the universe will be gone in a heartbeat once you become master of your own life and body. You, then, become master of the universe that counts. Or, more exactly, you finally inhabit a sentient reality.

There is a compounding effect as the subconscious keeps being ignored, year after year and generation after generation. I saw it all through my life. It is why ideas are rejected out of hand so often. It is why we don't want to consider anything new. It is why we are in this pit of misery. It is why loyalty has gone down the drain over the last century. And, yet, we tell ourselves that everything is okay. Right.

Men's failure makes everyone miserable. We don't dare think too deeply (stupour) because we might tread on something that leads to reveal the debacle that men have been conditioned to avoid contemplating at all cost: the quickly interrupted version of coitus that is the common experience. Just like an animal.

Just think about it. Just think about a couple that goes through the same experience of coitus being a disappointing experience day after day, week after week, year after year. Neither will ever mention it. "It's just the way it is." It hangs there as the relationship fades. No one will bring up the subject. I guess the woman may attempt to bring it up early in a relationship but, then, learns (often quite painfully) that it is not an acceptable subject and leads to horrible consequences. Just think what that does to the quality of the thoughts that remain for both.

Details

Leading into Details

I will warn you, right up front, it is going to sound difficult to love a woman the way both men and women desire. I will emphasize that it is *not* difficult for a human. It is difficult for an animal that has not yet used his brain to any serious extent. It is part of being human. As we learn how easy it is to transform the act of coitus into a loving event, we will become human. As men learn to master their bodies, they will not have the insane misbelief that they need to be masters of the universe. If any are meant to be masters of the universe, it will be the human race.

All of the books that I have written over the last twelve years are about the fact that men never learned that they can transform the act that creates life into an act that also creates love. The lack results in damage to the human race's development as a sentient race. *A sentient race would realize it is possible.*

The male *gender*, *not a few individuals*, needs to learn that all men can learn to love - easily. It is crucial to the man's sentience and the fulfillment of our sentient state. It needs to become firmly implanted into the brain of the human species. In other words, the human consciousness must become certain of the fact and certain of its humanity, decisively leaving the animal behind.

Have you had "that talk" with your father yet? How did it go? Did he fumble around and never say anything of import? Was he utterly relieved when you told him, "it's okay, dad, I know all about it." You didn't and neither did he.

Don't hold it against him. I'm not sure any man has really known how to love a woman physically before. They've usually known what the animal passed on to us. Rut. Stick it in and get it over with. Maybe think about baseball. Some may have actually stumbled on a way to last long enough. That is not the same as the human potential to completely understand the situation and overcome the limitations of the animal with full awareness and knowledge of what is going on. That is sentient.

I am all about simplifying what I am trying to say. Even so, it is just such a complicated picture (not these details, just the whole skewed sexual perceptions). We have been taught wrong about essentially everything for three thousand years. It has taken me writing eleven books to clearly understand thoroughly and explain. I am on my twelfth and final book.

The easiest part is to understand how to love a woman physically in the most elegant manner of the loving, human version of coitus. It is a version of coitus that only a sentient being could ever visualize or enact. It is only the implications, obfuscations, and refutations regarding this uniquely human, sentient experience that has made it so complicated.

The saying goes that men want sex and women want love. That portrays the dilemma poorly. Men *settle* for sex, in utter frustration, because they have not been able to fulfill the act of love the way they have always desperately desired to do and Nature always intended as a uniquely sentient experience.

This is about how a man learns he can last long enough to make coitus a loving, human, sentient, fulfilling event. This is about how a man learns that he is not held hostage by an animal's instincts, low grade thinking, and a dim-witted approach to life. This is all about how a man learns that he is sentient and human, not just an animal hiding from his humanity.

A man does not differentiate himself from an animal until he realizes that he can love. That is unique to human affairs. Loving coitus bridges the gap to the completed sentient state. A man doesn't learn to love fully until he can express that love in its physical form in the way Nature provided for a sentient race. Anything less is a disappointment. It is the only purely human sexual act. Eye to eye, celebrating life and love. Beneath all of the brainwashing, men *know* they can do better.

Early male humans equated themselves with animals and conducted themselves as such. They took a craven approach to life that has remained, in great part, to this day. We have yet to achieve a sentient state of awareness as long as we fail to make coitus a human, loving event.

Today's male humans remain mystified by their failure. They have accepted it as such because that is how it has always been. They have justified what has no justification. The leap to see beyond the paradigms that broke our humanity are formidable.

The act itself is simple.

I've learned a lot since the initial insight of "Don't twerk or jerk until the lady sings" and made it all available in some of the books starting with *Millennium*. This is the most thorough.

We are not human until the male gender learns to love.

Details

Number one. A man is not tied to a countdown clock in any way when it comes to coitus. That mistaken belief has stopped the male gender in its tracks since the beginning. It stopped men from ever investigating seriously. The belief is that, once you are aroused and penetrate, the ejaculation process is off and running. That is true for an animal and as long as we believe it is the best we can do, we remain an animal. It is not true of a human. Only exhaustion can intervene. It shouldn't get to that.

The huge mistake, compounded by that belief, is that the best you can do is hold on for dear life as you helplessly watch the tidal wave of ejaculate makes its way downstream. Let me be crystal clear. Any way in which you attempt hold back the tide, once it has begun, is bad. It can cause damage.

So, no, you are not on a clock and it is not a good idea to try to hold back the process of ejaculation, once begun in earnest.

Maybe the most important insight is that a man must learn to prevent the process from ever starting until he wants it to begin.

There is an alternative until you learn to control yourself. If you sense it early enough, you can stop all activity long enough for things to settle down. Some refer to this as edging. It works. Keep it in your toolbox for making love, but don't expect to use it except as you are learning to master your body.

What really works is to understand why the process of ejaculation gets started and what can be done about it so that you become a master of your own body. It's not magic. It's the sex glands. You are only held back by the witless instincts of an animal. We have never investigated any of it seriously.

There is only one thing that gets the ejaculation process started. Squeezing the sex glands in the bottom of your crotch, your pelvic region. *That* begins the process. Nothing else.

What happens is that the glands gets squeezed by two events, pelvic muscle contractions or the musculoskeletal structure in the pelvic region. They are two distinctly different mechanisms.

That squeezing can be avoided. They are squeezed due to one of two instincts of an animal without you ever realizing it.

There is one condition in which there is no stopping it. It will not be stopped if the glands are overfull. It is already being squeezed by being overfull. The solution is obvious.

Otherwise, two primary instincts cause the beginning of the end. One is simple to understand and control. That is the effect of the musculoskeletal structure on the pelvic region. The other is overcome by mastering the pelvic muscles of your body (the muscles in the pelvic region). It's not difficult to do.

It was only difficult to unravel from the misunderstandings. For an animal, it is impossible. You are not an animal.

The easy one is the musculoskeletal structure of the pelvic region. There is a desire to immediately plunge as deeply into that heavenly place, as you can. Save it for the grand finale. Doing so forces the musculoskeletal structure around the pelvic region into a position to squeeze the glands. It is best to remain as shallow as possible until you learn what you are doing.

As you become familiar, you will learn how deep, before the final plunge, is safe. The woman's stimulation only takes about two inches. Save the deep plunge for when she is ready.

All of the woman's erotic nerve endings are within two inches or less of the opening, anyways. The erogenous zone with the most erotic nerve endings is the clitoral nub which is located about half an inch *outside* of the vagina. This is critical. If you do no stimulate this clitoris button, it is unlikely you will be stimulating the woman enough to achieve own orgasm. More details later. It depends on how distant the nub is.

The other instinct is more difficult to comprehend and will take some serious effort for the first few that succeed. The muscles in your crotch are rather unique.

The more I study it, the more convinced I become that within two or three generations, without all of the impediments that are currently thrown into our faces, all the bad habits acquired, the missing knowledge, and the expectation of failure, combined with a growing confidence by the male gender, will make it as easy as learning to ride a bike. It is just a different effort.

You have to teach yourself to master those muscles and not use them during coitus. They are not involved in movement in any way and, yet, we flex them anyways because we never realized it triggers ejaculation. It is not difficult. It is just that we never tried before because we always veered away from any thoughts on the matter due to the paralyzing fear of admitting failure.

The muscles in your crotch, your pelvic muscles, will squeeze the sex glands if flexed. *That starts the process.* *They don't need to flex.* Those muscles only contract because we never think about it. We react like an animal without thought. Animals flex those muscles because they have the wit of, well, an animal.

The pelvic muscles have nothing to do with movement and, yet, during the mindless animal event of coital engagement, they contract and relax because *we don't think about it.* Instincts of the animal intervene. We never trained the muscles to be under our command. We never realized we didn't need to flex them.

It's easy to prove. Try moving any part of your body by using only your pelvic muscles. You can't do it. They are not attached in that way. They are not muscles for movement. That is not their purpose. They are attached in a way that controls the output of bodily fluids. In the case of ejaculate, flexing the pelvic muscles, during tumescence (hard-on), will invariably start the process of ejaculation by squeezing the sex glands.

During coitus, you have to learn to move your body *without* contracting the pelvic muscles. It's not really a big deal, once you become familiar with the idea. It's not like trying to master the heart muscles (which also can be done to some extent; i guess some may even be able to stop their heart completely. it's just that you never hear about it because they are dead).

The pelvic muscles are not needed at all during coitus. It is just a matter of learning to move the body without allowing those muscles to flex. It may be helpful to use them when the woman says it's time to end it, but I am not at all certain that it will ever be necessary. A deep dive is the best, most satisfying, and certain trigger. The positioning of the musculoskeletal structure for the deep dive is a nearly unavoidable trigger, which is why it is so commonly used before it is necessary.

This is why I came up with the phrase early on, "don't twerk or jerk until the lady sings." It's trite but it gets many points across. It points out, for instance, the most critical necessary point of control for the pelvic muscles. The word 'jerk' emphasizes that, when changing directions, especially on the backstroke (when you are withdrawing) it is *very* easy to let those muscles contract until well-trained. There is a tendency to jerk.

It is also a combined effort. In other words, the deeper you go, the easier it is for the pelvic muscles to inadvertently squeeze the sex glands in the crotch because you musculoskeletal structure is already closing on the area to be squeezed.

There is a third effect that needs to be considered but it is just a different part of mastering the muscles, and not nearly as difficult. That is the erotic sensation. This is the only way the head of the penis gets involved. The erotic sensations that blow your mind can trigger a spasming contraction of those muscles.

In essence, it is no different than the tickling sensation in other parts of your body. You can master the spasming by exercising those muscles, making them more supple and responsive rather than spasming with no control. Don't freak out. It should not take more than a couple of minutes a day to train them, maybe less for someone that matures into his sexuality already knowing what to do. Those muscles, otherwise, learn spasming best.

Those muscles, essentially, have never been consciously under a man's command or trained to become more supple and responsive. You can control the muscles reaction to tickling in any part of the body, if necessary. (i had a cruel older sister. i know). You can control any tickling sensation. If anything, it makes the experience enhanced and more mind-blowing.

The most mind-blowing part, though, is loving a woman right.

Once you master those muscles, some intriguing possibilities begin to present themselves. As I mentioned, the erotic zones of the woman are all very close to the opening. The most important, the clitoral nub, is about a half-inch outside and above the vagina. This nub, or button, has far more erotic nerve endings than even the head of your penis.

The distance from the vagina opening varies some. The closer it is to the vagina opening, the easier the woman is stimulated.

Without stimulating this, it is unlikely you will bring the woman to the point of orgasm. One has to pay attention in order to stroke the nub because of its position. One has to position oneself in such a way to stroke outside and above the vagina with the shaft of the penis. Make sure you know if you are stimulating acceptably. I have often wondered if this is actually the main reason that women take so long to achieve orgasm.

The rest of the clitoral erogenous zone, the clitoral wishbone, surrounds the vagina just inside the walls of its opening. This is the second most important erotic zone for the woman.

Stimulating the clitoris nub is mostly about positioning so that the shaft of your penis strokes it.

While it is not a challenge to stroke with the shaft, bringing the head of the penis into contact with the clitoral wishbone is another level of stimulation for the woman. Do not even attempt it until you have mastered the basics discussed above.

Bang! You are now human. You should be able to learn to last as long as *she* desires. You can finally feel successful at the most transcendent act of human life. You can love.

I wish I could be around for the next hundred years or so, as all of this flourishes. I just know there are mountains more learning that will occur once men's terrible inhibitions, frustrations, and emasculations are shredded as loving coitus truly and finally becomes celebrated as it always should have been and is transformed into a loving art form.

A couple of thoughts about how to make it easier. One way to avoid the musculoskeletal structure issue is to avoid movement in the pelvic region at all. As an example, moving the whole body instead prevents any need to twerk even slightly. Another possibility is to let the woman do all of the movement. I'm really not sure this is easier but it is something to consider.

I've had many women mention how it is all about the missing affection in men that is the problem. That is what drives women crazy and away. What women have never realized is that missing affection stems from this same problem that men have inadvertently buried for more than three millennia.

How can a man not become inhibited in his expression of affection and love as he fails at the most essential act of making love? How can a man maintain an affectionate demeanor when failing to express it in the most meaningful way in bed?

The man can feel utterly disappointed in the situation, as well as himself, feeling like he has already betrayed the woman he desires to show his love. Many a man will close up, once his failure to express his love in the most meaningful physical manner begins to sink in. It sinks in so insidiously many never even become aware of it. It has been around so long that it is masked in so many ways that no one notices. It can become a haunting feel that won't go away but, also, won't surface.

Yes, some overcome the shock. Some find other ways. You cannot tell me they are not disappointed all the same. You cannot tell me the inability to love face to face does not offend.

I'll stress again. It does not mean coitus has to be the only act of sex ever. It just cannot remain an outlier.

I mentioned exercises earlier. It is in some detail below. There are also plenty of Kegel exercises available on the web. Just keep in mind that there are two parts to the exercise. The second will not be mentioned in any reference to Kegel exercises or sexercises. Neither usually discriminates regarding the pelvic muscles. The first is to exercise those muscles to make them supple and responsive, under your command. The *second*, the one that is easy to miss, is to *not* flex those now supple muscles while exercising the muscles that are *meant* for movement in your thighs, torso, etc. in order to become familiar with the separation of efforts. I also like my exercises better because they only take a couple of minutes.

Regarding masturbation (I explain more below) it is crucial that we open our eyes and realize the potential for damage to the act of coitus. It is another case where men most likely avoid thinking about it, even as they do it.

Do not abuse your member. That is worse than any other bad habits you can pick up. On bad habits, do not let the habit of thinking only about your own orgasm during masturbation prevent you from concentrating on the woman's orgasm during the actual event of coitus. That is what it is all about.

Your main goal *has* to be the woman's orgasm during coitus. You orgasm is assured, hers is not. Habits are hard to break.

I have left much of my original details below because I am concerned that this is a difficult enough subject as it is. Reiteration in different words may help.

Original Details

Men have always accepted that starting the process of ejaculation was impossible to avoid. Because of this misconception, it became a matter of attempting to *stop the end result.* **_Big mistake._** That is far too late. The train has left the station. It became something similar to an olympic event in most men's minds. More strength is not the answer. More control is. In fact, using the muscles in the crotch is part of the problem.

The big picture is that the sex glands in the crotch, when squeezed, begin ejaculation. Nothing else. That's it.

Two instincts trigger the sex glands by squeezing them during tumescence (hard on). It has been 'a mystery' before now. So much for that mystery. Sorry, it still just pisses me off.

Men have only learned to hold on for dear life *after* the process of ejaculation has already begun. That assures the two or three minute limit that 'sex studies' always encounter. A study of the anatomy and the characteristics of the act of coitus is much more enlightening. There is no limit. There is no mystery, except the transcendent experience of sharing orgasm.

The unfortunate results of uncontrolled ejaculation ends the act of coitus before it can ever become a loving, thereby, human event that creates the loving environment that is necessary to fulfill our humanity. Uncontrolled ejaculation is a disaster. Until we can take command of our muscles, we are not human.

By studying the anatomy in the context of erection, ejaculation as well as some of the odd results of masturbation, it becomes clear. Squeezing the sex glands in the pubic area (i.e. the crotch, the pelvic region) begins the process of ejaculate discharge. The crotch muscles and musculoskeletal structure are the cause.

There are two instinctual reactions that cause the witless squeezing of the sex glands in the crotch. They are nothing more than the instincts of the animals that came before us.

That knowledge has been shunted aside due to the overwhelming feelings of shame and perplexity of resolution that were first encountered by the first fully aware sentient intellect more than three millennia ago. Instincts, when the shame is set aside and the intellect finally assesses the real situation, are easily overcome because we are human, thinking creatures.

One of those instincts is as simple to overcome as it is to understand. Men don't twerk until the lady sings. Thrusting the pubic bone (crotch) forward to the furthest extent squeezes the glands decisively (i.e. twerking). The animal's *instinct* is to immediately plunge as deeply as possible. Save it for later.

In the case of twerking (undisciplined full forward thrust), the musculoskeletal structure forces the pubic bones into a position that squeezes the sex glands. It will invariably cause the beginnings of orgasm, and ejaculation in the man's case.

The second instinct is more subtle. The pelvic muscles *are not involved and, thereby, not required, during movement.* The pelvic muscles also, when flexed, can squeeze the sex glands. The pelvic muscles do not *need* to flex, unless desired, during the movements of sexual activity. When flexed, they squeeze the sex glands. They have nothing to do with movement.

The other muscles in the thighs, buttocks, back, and torso, etc are the only muscles for movement. The crotch muscles only flex due to the witless instincts of the animal. They don't do anything regarding movement. They are not used for movement, we have just witlessly followed the instincts of an animal.

It is just a matter of realizing this and avoiding using the pelvic muscles for the movements involved in loving coitus. This is what I term 'jerking'. It just takes practice.

The two endpoints of the stroke are the most likely to cause those muscles to flex inadvertently, which is where the term jerking originated. The most difficult of the two to control, is the backstroke, when you are moving out, not in.

It's not so much leaving them lax as *not flexing them*. Flexing and relaxing those muscles acts like a pump on the glands. The 'tickling' effect on the head of the penis cause the same results through spasming. Mastery of these muscles is key.

The muscle response (jerking) or deep plunge (twerking) squeezes the glands containing the fluids that begins the cascade to orgasm. Save the deep plunge for the finale, when *she* is ready. It will *always* cause ejaculation and orgasm on call within a very short period of time. You can learn how long, also, with practice. It can all be under your command.

Don't *twerk* or *jerk* until the Lady sings, so to speak.

Holding on for dear life is *exactly* what a man does *not* want to do as it amounts to *flexing the pelvic muscles*!

One additional critical point. If the glands are <u>already overfull</u>, squeezing the glands is unavoidable. The solution is obvious.

Only about two inches is required to stroke the woman's every erotic nerve-ending inside and out, while allowing the head of the penis to remain fully inside the vagina. The shaft itself strokes the most sensitive arousal point (i.e. clitoral nub) that is just *outside* and *above* the opening (by ~ one-half inch or less). The other major erogenous zone for a woman is the clitoral wishbone, much less than two inches inside on both sides

Stroking the clitoral wishbone, just inside the vaginal opening, with the flaring portion of the head will also help stimulate the woman. That may be best saved for after you have learned the basics. The woman's twerking should assist her orgasm in the same way as a man. The two should discuss what works best.

Think on this. Now, once you both begin to achieve orgasm, you can leave the lights on and look into each other's loving eyes as you each achieve the transcendent state of orgasm. The only sin and shame to sex is that we have not been able to do this before. Turning out the lights proves the issue.

Just be careful and go very slow until you understand 1) how deep is safe (it should be far more than an inch or two once you progress in your learnings) and 2) how to avoid contracting (or, worse, spasming) the muscles in the crotch.

An additional technique, if necessary, is to stop all activity at the first sign that you are becoming overstimulated until the sense of overstimulation is gone. It should not be necessary with exercise and practice but may be useful while still learning.

It is a learning process. We are human. That is what we do. That is what we are *supposed* to do. In the case of coitus, we have avoided the learning process, thus remaining a dumbfounded animal.

These points are straightforward and will become as natural as the instincts and animal responses that they replace within a generation or two of the time that humanity begins to succeed at love in its most essential physical form. Little real learning should be necessary within a generation or two.   It will be absorbed from the confidence of one's elders (which is completely absent today) and, maybe, a few minor insights that will be commonly known, like, "don't twerk, don't jerk, and exercise. Become familiar with the muscles in the crotch and *don't flex them*. Make them supple through exercise."

Exercise

The exercises are just as crucial for loving coitus in youth as it is for later in life. There are other benefits as you age, like not wearing diapers. The immediate advantages, even in youth, include making it easier to master the muscles and any untoward spasming of the muscles. It will take some slight effort and discipline, as well as exercise (two minutes!), to make them supple and avoid flexing and spasming. Avoiding the deep plunge is just a matter of paying attention. Now, you will be able to open your eyes to the one you adore while actually loving her in the best way possible.

I spend around *two* minutes (only two!) exercising those muscles daily, and, also, practicing *not* flexing them in a separate set of exercises in which I only exercise the muscles that *are* necessary for movement.

On your back with knees bent and swinging towards each other and away works well. Flex the pelvic muscles as you swing the knees towards each other. Relax the muscles as you swing the knees apart. Thirty times or approximately thirty seconds. This will help you become familiar with the muscles and make them supple. Then, hold them flexed for a count of five, six times while swinging the knees in and, then, leaving the loose as the knees move away from each other. Then, repeat both exercises, but leave the pelvic muscles relaxed in both directions of movement of the knees. Work only the leg, butt, and hip muscles to become familiar with the pelvic muscles remaining relaxed while the other muscles flex and relax. This could also be practiced during walking, sitting, or any form of exercise. Just don't get that far off look in your eyes. Just kidding, I think.

Another good, errr, non-exercise is standing knee bends *without* flexing the pelvic muscles.

In essence, you are trying to do two things. Condition the pelvic muscles *and* become familiar with *not* using them when it is unnecessary and detrimental to the act of loving coitus.

I really doubt this will be the last written on exercises to make it easier to avoid untimely orgasms. I have already rewritten this a dozen times as I learned more and more. I expect there will be much more discovered as we remove the blinders.

Self-stimulation

Everything I have written has been about removing the stigma from coitus and sex completely. So, I am not going to avoid discussing self-stimulation as if it didn't ever happen.

Another caution. Self-stimulation (or dress rehearsals, or masturbation, if you prefer) needs to be done carefully for the man. If you abuse your member, it will come back to haunt you. *Do not inadvertently do so!* It will make it almost impossible to avoid the beginnings of ejaculation. There is no reason to abuse your member, *if you realize what triggers an orgasm.*

This is also one of the key insights that led me through all of this. During self-stimulation it can be difficult to achieve orgasm. Obviously, something is different. At least two things, actually (maybe there are more). One is that the twerking doesn't usually happen. Secondly, a person cannot cause their own ticklish, sensual response. So, the possibility of spasm is reduced. A person cannot tickle themselves. I'm guessing we have a lot more to learn in this area. I learned, in the distant past, to control the ticklish response under the arms for entirely different reasons. The same applies. The twinge spasming can be under your command with ease in the case of coitus. I controlled a far more intense tickling under the arms (which was the reason I had to learnt to do so).

This just adds to the surprise when a young man first experiences coitus. What could last forever during masturbation can be over in seconds during coitus. Can you see how this helped me figure out what was going on? It sure wasn't anything I read on the web that helped.

Abuse, which can happen in attempts to rush to completion, will make the spasm response *extremely* difficult to overcome. *Do not abuse your member.*

Humanity should learn to approach masturbation unabashedly. It is far better than letting the lack of release get under one's skin. It is best limited to assuring the avoidance of embarrassing situations but, just like our repression of sex, it is, in fact, harmful to act like no one does it or that it is cursed. I'm not expecting that to change in a hurry. Once we lose our sense of shame regarding sex, maybe we will have a chance.

Circumcision

Don't let your child (either sex, really) be mutilated by circumcision. In the U.S., many think it is a Christian tradition. IT IS NOT A CHRISTIAN TRADITION!!!! The health aspect is also a crock. It is sadism. It leaves mental scars.

There is no rational reason for the mutilation of circumcision (either gender), though there are many irrational, insane reasons.

A circumcised person can still achieve controlled ejaculation but it may be more of a challenge (I was circumcised).

More importantly, the biggest thing for me is that I am certain it leaves a psychic shock when they slice it away, no matter the anesthetics or sharpness of the scalpel. There's just no need for it. It is sick and sadistic. It is an animal reveling in causing pain.

I would say that, no matter where you are in the world, it would be worth checking before you have a baby. In many places (the U.S. south), they will slice without asking.

Summary

Just remember, you are human. Of course you can control the muscles and your own discharge. Keep in mind that overfull glands means they *will* be squeezed and it will be over in a hurry. How you handle that is up to you.

Be sure you are familiar with the female anatomy regarding this subject. More than the anatomy, be familiar with the woman's wants and needs in this area, as well.

Do not become discouraged if it takes a little while to adjust and make things work. At this point, it is all new. The older you are, the more time should be expected in order to adjust as there are more bad habits necessary to overcome.

I will be surprised if young men have much difficulty at all.

You can now proceed to engage in loving coitus, that is, mutual orgasm, enthusiastically in a human manner while gazing into your lover's eyes with the lights on. Love can finally mature into its sentient form. We can become human. Rather than a porn-watching subhuman race that obsesses about sex because it is an animal's failure. I apologize for concentrating on the men's issues but men have the most to learn, by far.

There is another point that I have not highlighted before. The closest I came was mentioning that, after men gain their confidence, their self-respect, the rest will come easily.

While that is true, it is not enough, at this point. During the transition into that state, there are a few things that a man will need to consider. After we are human, it will be as obvious as the Earth beneath your feet.

Not only does a woman's orgasm take some time but, at least at this point, so does arousal for many women. I think it is very possible that this, also, will change, once women become convinced that they, also, can expect to achieve orgasm during coitus on a consistent basis and men realize the required nuances. Their enthusiasm may often even match that of the man.

The point is that, at this time, if a man does not take time, effort, and knowledge achieving the woman's high arousal, before beginning coitus, she may never achieve orgasm. I would love to see a book by a woman on these matters. The orientation for a man needs to change radically. It is not all about him. It is all about loving and giving, not just pleasing oneself. That destroys everything that is human in a person.

For women, just make sure you are doing the opposite of what I've recommended for men and you should orgasm easily. Flex and twerk like crazy or as much as he can bear, which should improve over time. Relish the erotic feelings that cause the spasms to engage. Again, I would dearly love to see a woman write a book on the woman's sexual situation and insights.

I am becoming more and more convinced that, as we open up and become more comfortable with the change and the insights, we will learn a lot more in every area of our existence.

All of this will become natural once we remove the blinders. We will no longer be cringing in a corner, and we will see further ways in which to improve. I don't mean just the physical aspects.

This book will become unnecessary soon. It should become such an easily understood success, once we have rid ourselves of the millennia of nonsense, that reading will not hold much value.

I have always suggested that it will take about three generations, or one hundred years, to become completely adapted from the time it is accepted. I guess what I mean by 'accepted' is that it has, as Maxwell Gladstone puts it, reached the 'tipping point'. That enough of humanity has accepted and proved the case, and it begins to move forward with a will. From that point, three generations, maybe less.

As an example of the other aspects to explore further, I'll mention romance and, of course, foreplay. Those are other natural aspects of being human that have been inhibited by men's inability to love physically, just like the inhibited affection. I'll just say that romance should span a lifetime, not just long enough to get woman bedded, as is often the case today. This will happen naturally as men learn how to love.

Once our natural desire to love is established and reinforced by men gaining confidence that they can love, the rest of our loving nature will flourish. This goes well beyond the intimate relationship, as well. Humanity can become a balanced, emotionally stable, rational loving race of sentient beings without the mindless paranoia, hopelessness, and despair.

A few further notes as I progress even further. First of all, after six books I am annoyed to find that the excellent term that I had created, indefinitely delayed ejaculation, 1) is not unique, and 2) has been already adopted to cover the case of the poor man that can't ever ejaculate or, goodness forbid, might last long enough to pleasure his woman with orgasm.

Secondly, there is a lot better term: controlled ejaculation or ejaculation on command. I don't really care. Just need a term.

I haven't even touched on any of the subjects besides men lasting long enough that are crucial to making love. The rest of it will come easily, once men are certain that they don't need to fail at the most essential task: lasting long enough.

The rest is easy, if you consider it at all, but still worth noting. The emotional loving, the affectionate responses and attitudes; the romance, the foreplay, the loving attitude, the gentle, equitable treatment of women, true equality that is celebrated, not legislated, the rainbow loving of women that has been lacking, all falls right out of what I have been explaining. Once men put their shame behind them.

Also, remember, it is the woman that gets pregnant, not you. So, if coitus is off the table, for any reason, deal with it. If you care for her enough, you'll stick around. Find some other way in which to achieve mutual orgasm. That is the whole point. The *inability* of men to overcome the coital failure is what it is all about. Not the actual act itself. If men can, that's all that counts.

Admissions and extensions

In the meantime, though, as we seek our way, it is at least worth mentioning a few key points and new ... I'd call them insights but a better term would be investigations. They are not proven. I am way too old to confirm any more insights.

Everything above in this chapter has been proved to my own satisfaction. It was more difficult than most any man should encounter from this point forward. That is the point in explaining all of this. The effort is not difficult, just overcoming the brainwashing and avoidance of the issue was difficult.

In a number of ways, it was more difficult for me. I had no template. I was encumbered by all of the lies, misdirections, and utter suppression of the subject that have burdened mankind for millennia. I understand the fury that percolated within me for that last twelve years and is evident in my previous books. It was necessary in order to break through all of the nonsense. It was like a fire burning all of the lies, delusions, and paradigms.

I have now provided a basic template to move forward and avoid the pitfalls that I encountered over a lifetime *before* I realized it was a sham almost too late in life.

I realize this does not prove the case for all men. That will take some time and effort by others to show that it is not an isolated case and expand on the basic template that I have provided. I just want to emphasize that I am no one special when it comes to making loving coitus. In fact, there were multiple additional handicaps to my situation.

Everything I have to add, from this point forward, regarding improving men's performance has no proof to speak of, other than I have spent the last dozen years pondering it all and linking many, many obscure dots.

These insights came far too late for me to prove them out with any level of certainty. I have no proof they help but they are reasonable considerations and extrapolations from previous insights *that did work.* Some, points below, are just clarifications.

Humanity never stops improving on anything that it (finally) takes seriously instead of hiding away in a corner somewhere.

Loving coitus will become far more than the clinical analysis that I have had to provide. It will become loving art. It will expand the art of loving into something more human, once the unnecessary fear and shame are put away. It is far more natural than riding a bike. More like learning to communicate.

None of this I explain will be necessary at all as men begin to gain confidence in their ability to love.

It's just that hangover from delusion for three millennia that continues to concern me. The more thorough the explanation, the easier it may be for men to get over the hurdle of fear that prevented the human race from loving fully.

On the topic of exercise, I want to stress *not* to follow any rule book, including mine. Actually, that goes for everything. Rule books are for animals. Start with my suggestions but find what works best for you. I would be shocked in the extreme if people don't find even better ways to strengthen and train those muscles and make it all even easier. If they are sentient, they should certainly be looking for better alternatives or, at least, ones that suit them better. We think. That's what we do.

I lost along the way through the many books one interesting technique that can be used while learning to master one's body. Moving the whole body, rather than flexing the hips in any way, or not moving any portion of the *man's* body are two ways to avoid squeezing those glands. I'll leave it for your exploration.

Sometimes I think of it like this door that men have always considered locked against them. Now, as we push gently against it, we find it is wide open. Quit letting the fears that your ancient ancestors handed down prevent you from realizing you are a human. You can love a woman the way you have always desired.

One of the most crucial points that I cannot emphasize enough is that it is about a man changing his focus and, thereby, his behaviour from that of an animal to that of a human. That is the real point of all of this. Men's humanity has been hampered.

The laser focus for every man needs to become that it is about *sharing* the love in its physical form. All of the myriad forms of love can flourish from that point forward.

This is where the discussion becomes more speculative. As I mentioned with twerking, it is the whole musculoskeletal structure that kicks in to squeeze those glands in your crotch during tumescence. There may be other ways the musculoskeletal structure can be persuaded to avoid pressure on those glands. Just a crazy idea.

Men often have a tendency to point their feet at an angle with the toes away from each other. I think there is a distinct possibility that one's toes being closer together than one's heels or, at least, parallel might very well cause the musculoskeletal structure to become less prone to squeezing the sex glands. It seems like it may make more room for the glands.

More so, as I studied it further, it strengthens the muscles on the inside of the thigh if one walks with the toes pointed slightly inward. I don't know but I am hoping someone will try.

I have another exercise that I do. It is bending at the hips while standing with the legs and back straight. When doing the exercise with the toes closer together than the heels, I can feel those back, inner thigh muscles stretching. I am beginning to believe it is possible that these muscles also need to be strengthened in order to make it easier to avoid using the crotch muscles during coitus. Just a theory. Errr, hypothesis.

This, by the way, is a perfect example of where my age limits me. Make no mistake, as you age, your bones harden. That not only made this study a challenge. It made it painful. To the point I had to quit the investigation.

A final note as I look at men attempting to love a woman. Another key aspect that may always cause the woman to take so long to achieve orgasm is the location of the clitoris nub. Unless it is extremely close to the vagina opening, it may very well be that many men never stroke it during coitus.

(yes, i realize I am repeating myself. i'm not *that* old!)

So, not only is it a matter of men lasting long enough but, maybe just as importantly, that they do not realize how to stimulate the woman to orgasm. In other words, the combination should knock everyone's socks off.

Labyrinth

I was just listening to "I'm so in love with you" by Texas. Amazing. I never gave up on that dream. Or, as Sade phrased it so eloquently, I am a "Soldier Of Love". It's funny. So many songs give it away. We are just not listening.

I took the Soldier of Love job very seriously. I wasn't accepting the scraps left on the table by the animal. I could never accept that we are so horrible at love. Big love, little love, we are terrible every step of the way. It all begins with lousy coitus. Our current terrible rendition of a sentient existence has a beginning, a source. Lousy coitus. Loving coitus will transform.

There's something about sharing this form of love with another that releases love in all its forms. It is just that very fundamental to our existence as a sentient life form. Sentience learns to love.

It is just wrong that we accept the paltry remnants left by the animal. The link between puberty and the loss of innocence gives it all away. Love is initiated through the act of loving. As it stands, we accept a stunted, damaged interpretation of love because the act of love remains nothing of the sort. Coitus is only loving when it is shared, in all aspects. Its lack shunts our humanity and sentience into limbo. We do not "grow up" today. We grow disillusioned, bitter, and deprived of love.

Our forefathers were at a loss. There was too much baggage, because we evolved from an animal that was incompetent at the most intimate act of caring for a billion years before we arrived on the scene. The inertia of the animal has held sway ever since.

The animal doesn't care because it can't do a thing about it. We do care. We sense there is something more because of our conscious awareness. Sentient clarity can prevail. It must.

Maybe, instead of love, I should use the term, self-actualization. I worry that the word love is too full of false innuendoes. But, I'd rather be blunt at this juncture. We do not know how to love and it is critically important to a race of beings that can create untold damage in a lesser state.

As these thoughts rumble through my mind, a different rage is beginning to take hold. It's not really new. It's been building since *Millennium*, but it has now hit its stride as I encounter people who certainly have read what I have to say and continue on the dumbfounded way of the prehuman. Not a word from anyone can be detected. Sorry. Hyperventilating. Onward.

Sentient beings are different. On one hand, we are aware that there *should* be more to coitus. On the other hand, we have remained convinced that we can't do anything about it. The latter dislodges our sentient clarity, honesty, and self-respect. That is so wholly the animal's confusion as to be glaring.

Nature provided for the transformation of coitus into a fulfilling event. For a sentient being, it is simple to do. All we have to do is open our eyes to our humanity, shut the animal up.

Love will become real for humanity, once we realize only the witless instincts of an animal have been holding us back. Any man can last as long as *she* pleases. Love begins there.

A man lasting long enough does not equate with love, of course. But, how is a man supposed to learn to love when he can't take the first step into the realm of love. Worse yet, how is he supposed to face his failure? *Knowing* that one can love another only opens the door to the possibility and closes the door on all of the unwarranted paranoia and self-doubt, the fear that we don't deserve our sentient state. We do. We just have to reach out and grasp it. That is enough to make love real.

The instincts of the animal are easy to overcome, once we realize they are only instincts, that they are not cast in stone. It just takes a little thinking, which I've done for you. It will release our humanity to become whole and loving.

It is only a matter of subordinating the instincts of the animal that make it impossible to last long enough to call it making love. We can talk all day about love but, if between the sheets, it doesn't happen, then love remains damaged and so do we.

Doesn't that give it all away to you? Can you see that all of our lunatic antics have a root cause, a source? A source that has no reason to continue to exist? The most direct conclusion is accepting that all forms of *shared* physical love are valid. But, there is one that supersedes them all. Coitus. It is different.

It makes life. It keeps us from going instinct. At this point, that may seem to some to be the best option, but that is just because you remain stuck in the prehuman existence that does not suffice for a sentient race.

Coitus is the form of loving that Nature created for the purpose of fulfilling humanity. It doesn't mean that everyone has to take part in it. There are good arguments for many choosing a different way but, still, for us to become fully human, coitus must become fully human. It's continued absence drives us crazy. It continues to force us to remain less than human. It split humanity into a million shards rather than a whole sentient race.

Where do you think all of the troubles of humanity originate? In the home, in the bed, where love and life-creation should merge into one and make us whole. The disturbance in the home radiates outward distorting all aspects of what should be an open, fulfilled race of sentient beings that embrace their existence rather than shun it. Our lack of consummating the most natural act of love destroys our sentient state. Nature always intended that we could learn to love and become human. We have not yet.

Loving coitus must become a certainty to humanity. No current definition of love describes all that love encompasses. The current definitions are vague, uncertain. The act of coitus must attain its sentient state of love. It must become an act of love, of sharing. Our sentience is established with the fulfillment of our desire to share loving in the form of coitus with another.

It is the defining difference that makes us human, that transcends the animal. It fulfills the advanced form of emotional context to match our advanced level of awareness. We become sentient in every way. Our heart becomes educated. Within a very few generations the act of loving coitus will become as natural as the instincts of the animal that it replaces.

Love in its fullest, human, sentient form leads to emotional stability, sanity, and reason. Anything less drives a sentient race mad. Just look around and admit the truth, finally.

Love is self-validation for a sentient race. Once we realize we can love, the entire picture of humanity changes radically. We will begin to self-actualize. Not just as individuals, but as a race.

Reason alone is enough to proves the case. We think. We can easily overcome the animal's instincts. We can become human.

We have been following the animal's lead since we first gained our sentience. It's time for that to change.

A Maze

It's not an option. We can't continue to run from our sentience, though that is exactly what we have done for millennia.

Loving coitus is the natural extension of life for a sentient race. It fulfills the newly developed Trajectory of Life provided by conscious awareness. A hurdle must be crossed for men to learn to love. Hiding from the shame and failure is not a viable option. We remain broken until we perceive with clarity.

The sentient realization that coitus is not complete was complicated by the relentless realization that *no* species (before humanity) can last very long at coitus. Because of that, our ancestors had to compromise. They were not comfortable enough with their sentience to deal with the problem. We are.

Our ancestors could not accept the huge difference between what a human expects from coitus and what an animal expects. It confounded them utterly. They handed down their confusion.

The animal has no expectations. Dumb animals can only follow their instincts and the urge for sexual release.

Sentient beings can overcome a dumb animal's stupour by thinking. That's what we do. We are sentient, human.

Our sentient state forces the awareness that cannot be denied. There is more to coitus. Until we do something about it, we remain less than human. That is why I use the term prehuman.

The crucial aspect of sentience is that perceptions have to makes sense. They have to correlate to a sentient reality. Clarity is an overriding concern for a sentient race equipped with conscious awareness and intellect. Anything less refutes our sentient state. The phrase, "perceptions are reality" is a swindle. If perceptions do not match a sentient reality, we remain in a deranged state. The act of coitus must achieve its sentient potential to achieve the status of clarity for a sentient race.

Because we are sentient, we know there is more to the act than rutting. It cannot be avoided. Attempting to do so forces us into a state of stupour. It is time to realize that unassisted loving coitus can be achieved. It is time to become a sane sentient race.

It is not the mystery that everyone thinks. We have remained in a stupour for three millennia while we developed the complex wherewithal to see through to the source of the problem *and* provide for a solution (i.e. Details). Nothing less is acceptable.

It was the details of making it work that were far beyond our earliest ancestors. It is the state of stupour that caused the maze.

We have been duped since the beginning. Our incredible potential is about to be revealed once we learn to love.

Loving coitus and its success is not a mystery. It is about the incredible feeling of orgasm - for both. It must be shared. It is the truest of blisses. It unlocks everything that has been missing for a highly developed sentient race. It is the fulfillment of the concept we call love. That is why we call it 'making love'.

Life in a teacup

Do you remember those days? I still can. That vibrant feeling to which I had looked forward for so long with mounting expectation and anticipation. The amazing feeling when looking into a woman's eyes in the naiveté of youth!

Later (sadly), after I 'grew up', I picked over the dusty ashes of my youth. Mystery to misery. As we continue to fail to succeed at loving coitus, each generation is convinced "it is time to grow up. It is time to put away all of the hopes and dreams of youth."

The older generation could never admit that they had failed to become human and loving and cherish that innocence. It was easier just to convince the next generation to remain broken.

What we seek is *not* the naive innocence of an animal but the informed innocence provided by a sentient race of beings' clarity and Nature's gifts that make loving possible, thus finally freeing us from the animal's limited scope.

Gosh, the thought of loving a woman! The pulse-pounding when I looked into certain women's eyes as the same look was reflected back at me. So much promise! All turned to ashes.

As I crossed the threshold of puberty, I began to realized something was awry. It took me fifty years to figure out what.

Loving a woman; to me, has always implied face to face. The idea of loving a woman was planted so firmly in my head that everything must turn out perfect, right?

All the romance movies and books talk about how fine it is to love a woman. Foolishly, I bought it all; hook, line, and sinker. The happily-ever-after was a given, right? Then puberty hit like a freight train. Vague feelings began to disturb me.

The shock of attaining puberty totally unprepared for the failure of loving coitus tore me apart. Confidence was dashed on the rocks of the animal's witless approach to coitus. Even then, though, I was conditioned to avoid the realization. The source of the disturbance, never acknowledged due to the millennia of conditioning, has built a formidable wall around the failure.

How could it be that three millennia after the humanity gained some level of wit, no one had prepared me for that utter failure? No answers were anywhere to be found. No one was willing to talk about it. No one was willing to admit that there was something wrong. "Grin and bear it" echoes down the millennia, through each generation. "Life is pain!" "Act like a *man!*"

But, still, it was going to be like magic! Right? Funny thing. The magic was missing. All the glory of loving was for naught.

What a shock! Everything was *not* okay! Research all I cared (I am very good at it) and the best I got was, "it's still a mystery! Good luck!" "Hold on with everything you've got!" Everything about being a *man* is about refuting his humanity. The evidence is clear on this, though I do not see the point in getting into it.

I'm sorry but I'm calling it right here and now. Our ancestors have acted like morons, right on down the line. There was probably very good reasons for it but, still. They blocked access to the crucial difference that makes us more than a demented animal. They blocked love and never even knew it.

I finally discovered that, not only was no one willing to talk about it, no one was willing to even think about it. No one was willing to confront the situation and either accept it or transform it. The moronic gods had spoken! Everyone shoves it into the attic of the minds with no consideration. "We are just animals" has also echoed down the corridors of our stupour.

The stupour of the animal has been in charge since the beginning. We just carried it along with us. We never accepted what our sentience was telling us. Men can learn to love. Men can overcome the instincts of an animal that make it all fail miserably. Our early ancestors rejected our sentience flat out. Later generations carried on in utter befuddlement and shame.

Our most ancient ancestors hid that which confounded them from themselves and their descendants. Then, they acted like everything was okay. "That's just the way it is," they proclaim and wipe their hands free of our humanity.

The animal's proclivities remain lurking in the subconscious due to a cover-up of monumental proportions regarding the utter failure of our sentient state to address this critical issue.

The cover-up proceeded to get more complicated and bizarre as sentient thought was tossed into the bin with prejudice. All that was left was the craftiness and spite of an animal.

The truth and a crucial question remained buried in our subconscious. "How come I'm the only one to get pleasure out of this most natural act of sex? What about the woman?" "How can I possibly call this act love until both are fulfilled?" No one was willing to ask those questions, even inside their own minds.

Look around. The disturbance runs deep, very deep.

Maybe the most disastrous and disturbing question some men ask themselves is, "Why do I have this problem? What about all the other guys?" It turns out that between 75% (official estimate) and 99% (my own estimate) of men have the same issue. To put it simply, we all have the same issue if we do not overcome the instincts of an animal that force the failure.

The limitations (i.e. instincts) were only imposed *on an animal*. They do not apply to a *thinking* human. We can overcome the animal's instincts that cause failure. The biggest challenge is the blinders of conditioning that force us not to look. I know it scares men spit-less to think about, but what other choice do men have? Continue to act like a wrecking ball to all of our humanity? Rescind Natures' offer for so much more?

I've shown how to overcome the issue. It can work for everyone, once we quit freaking out and realize just how important it is to transform the act of coitus into a loving act.

We are a sentient, highly intelligent, highly motivated race that can *think*. Nature provided resolution for a sentient race.

The pill is not resolution. The pill does not substitute for a man's humanity. If anything it digs the animal's trench deeper.

The desire for a pill, by the way, only emphasizes what we have hid with every breath since the beginning. Men want to share their love. They just never realized they can. All on their own without appendages, appliances, acrobatics, or pills.

Man's humanity is only unleashed by the self-actualization caused by conquering the animal's witless instincts that have held us back. The male gender must prove its humanity to itself by succeeding at unassisted loving coitus.

In the past, whenever the subject came up, it was crushed with a mountain. You can see the results of that decision we have followed all around you. We have inadvertently severely damaged sentient reality. It remains a warped animal's state. The fracture begins between the two genders and extends itself into the most ludicrous and foolish splinters of our existence.

The question that has never been seriously asked is ,"Why in can't I do significantly better than some animal?" Not by a minute, but as long as desired. *We can. We are human!!!!*

We even justified the animals' failure by declaring two or three minutes a success! The time interval means nothing without fulfillment of the loving of a woman. Three minutes doesn't. So, why do we attempt to justify failure? Because we are hiding.

Coitus can consistently be a loving act for the human race. It only becomes a loving act when both take full pleasure in it.

The clock that ends coitus in a hurry, and ruins any chance of love, can be suspended by a man for as long as *she* desires.

The most terrible, debilitating effect of the stupour we have endured because of this blindspot is that it changes men's perception of themselves in oh, so many awful ways.

The inability to supersede the animal has crushed men's spirit for millennia. They remain convinced they are no better than an animal, undeserving of the sentient state. All because of a twisted, bizarre avalanche of inertia. This unmentioned issue has haunted the whole human race since the beginning.

All of the bizarre, manic, preposterous behaviours of the male gender of the human race has a source. They can be eliminated in less than a generation.

Radiant by Degrees

I am going to start with a statement that I won't even attempt to explain. It regards the future. It is the one aspect of a sentient future of which I feel fairly certain.

We only feel so alone because we have not attained our sentient state of mind. That isolates us, just like an animal. We should be sharing a sentient reality. That fulfills another need.

The title for this chapter was a whim. It just seemed right. Now, I know why. These twelve books are just the beginning. It has been a long hard process for me to winnow out all of the insane paradigms of the animal to even begin to get close to what is wrong and, more importantly as well as more difficult, to figure out what is right and explain with some attempt at clarity.

I keep digging and unearthing more. So, far, I've gotten to

Shared consciousness

My latest breakthrough is the implications of shared consciousness and *not* sharing it.

This is at the heart of all of our problems. While, whether we like it or not, there is a shared consciousness that coitus is not all it should be, we don't share it. It is an open secret that we dare not mention. That is why we remain isolated from one another.

Men have shut down that sharing because they cannot accept that they cannot make coitus a loving event.

That drives humanity to limit the conscious sharing to an extreme, insane degree. *Because* men cannot accept that they cannot (which they can; all they need to do is *try*) make coitus a loving event, they have not only broken the sharing of the loving event but, also, broke the shared consciousness. The ramifications of which I get into that further in Con Job below.

As long as we don't share our consciousness openly, we can never be fully sentient. We cannot share our consciousness openly until we have shared loving in its most natural form. Then, we are truly free. It is the liberation, the freedom, for which we have been waiting.

Do you see what I mean about radiant by degrees now? The mess we have created by carrying on like an animal rather than facing up to the mind-bending reality of sentience is built in so many layers that it will take many minds over more than one generation to see through it all. I'd like to believe that I could make it through all of the myriad confusion but it is becoming clearer and clearer that I have only swept the doorstep clear.

The Secret that isn't a secret

This is where it all began to fly apart for humanity. We need coitus to survive.   It's main requirement is to make babies. Because the other important requirement, *for a sentient race*, was so difficult to achieve (for our earlier, mindless ancestors), the question could not remain pending. It could not remain an open question.   It haunted our existence.   So, the *shared consciousness* created a hole in itself.   The secret that isn't a secret at all.

Everyone knows that prehuman men are lousy at coitus but no one wants to state it aloud.   The fear of inadequate coitus overwhelmed our better sense. No one is willing to even suggest that men can do better. Until now. Even if it didn't work (which it will), we cannot keep acting like it's some sort of secret. The open secret creates a gaping hole in our sentient state.

Broken innocence

That's the best way I can put it at this point.   Broken innocence. Our innocence should never be compromised. For a sentient race, facing issues and dealing with them in a rational manner preserves the innocence.   I refer to it as informed innocence. It is not the witless innocence of an animal.

The lack of loving coitus, because it is so obviously possible to a rational mind that is actually thinking and not cluttered with nonsense, compromises our innocence. We were not thinking rationally when men convinced themselves there was nothing to be done. We are still not thinking rationally.

The human race, so far, has only attributed sex to the end of innocence. That is not even close. The failed attempt to make coitus a loving event compromises our innocence. Sex is not the problem.   It is the absence of the most natural form of love-making and the blindspot of irrationality that it has caused.

There may still be some that desire alternatives for a variety of reasons but, once *loving* coitus becomes available, coitus will be even more popular than ever. As men become human, the final barrier will drop between the two genders. We will be on equality's doorstep. Perfectly aligned with that, the alternatives will become nothing more than another way to share one's love, when the most natural route is not available for some other reason than the male's lack.

It is the absence of the all-important loving coitus that has rocked our world (not in a good way) since day one.

Con Job

A con (confidence) man's job proves the case very well indeed. A conman learns to sound confident in something they know is entirely unjustified. Men have had lots of practice for millennia.

Men have been living the confidence game for the last three millennia. Men learned long ago to act and sound all confident in the face of the utter defeat of their humanity. Men learned to act confident, even though they could not love. That is the lesson that the male gender has been learning all along. Men *act* like they are human. Now, they need to *become* human.

Can you think of a more debilitating way to exist? Can you not see it in all of the footsteps of the male gender? The insanity of their situation is attempting to break loose, once more.

Humanity's problems

We only 'solve' humanity's problems by becoming human. The problems we attack are the problems of an animal attempting to *act* like a human, adjust to a sentient situation of shared awareness. With an animal, the witless acceptance of the failed coital engagement went no further than one's own mind. With humanity, we have tried to keep the same arrangement.

We act like there is nothing wrong with coitus, while the whole world (literally, today) blows up around us.

"No, everything is alright. Everything is just fine. W're okay."

We accept our awful conditions because we haven't had the insight to accept that we are due so much more. One blindspot kept us from even looking for something better. In its absence, everyone is caught in their own little nightmare.

In its presence, life becomes the dream we always expected. The dystopia, then, disappears.

Dystopia

Maybe I'm getting bitter as no one accepts the potential that I have laid out for all to see. Maybe I'm just tired of trying to explain to all and sundry. At the same time, I must say that I keep going deeper and deeper into my own understanding of what is wrong and what can be right. There is nothing left to unearth. I will not write another book on the subject. Well, maybe I will, if I get some damned help (that sharing I am mentioning throughout this book).

We are so caught up in our dystopia that we are beyond the bounds of realizing that the end of dystopia is not utopia.

Utopia, of course, is a foolish dream. We wholeheartedly believe dystopia is the lot in life for humanity.

Human Consciousness

It possible I have skipped over a key concept throughout the series of books. The realization has been with me so long that I have never really mentioned it to any extent.

There is something that I term Human Consciousness. This is not the consciousness of an individual human but the gathered, or combined consciousness of the human race. Right now, it is full of fabricated nonsense of detrimental value.

As I take it out and look at it, again, it is even far more important than my initial understanding. It also is unique in the annals of life on this planet. It is what will make us human, once we quit accepting all of the lies, delusion, and confusion.

We have a combined consciousness that shatters or directs our efforts. So far, it has been shattering them. The lies we have been fed, with one distorted view struggling against the others, bringing every form of propaganda (a lie by any other name) to dominate prehuman life, have never ended. All of the animal antics to dominate human life are all directed *away* from the most crucial lie that men remain desperate to hide.

If you look at it from an historical perspective, as I have had to do with all of this, it makes sense. As descendants of animals, we had no idea how to share consciousness. When put to the task, we immediately found we had something to hide. Our shared consciousness suffered but we were unfamiliar with the concept, so we thought nothing of it.

How to put in into words that you will understand? Unlike any life form before, our thoughts combine into something more than what an individual thinks. The most egregious, disgusting, and common thought that has always upset me no end is, "we are only human." It is the animal accepting defeat.

One term for that combined consciousness is The Great Conversation, though that usually implies only the thoughts of the 'great' thinkers. I use the term elsewise. It is the consciousness of humanity. It is closer to the concept of Gaia.

In its original context, it was pretty straightforward. Bewilderment in wonder and amazement about *everything*. As we progressed, it began to tentatively spread its wings. We passed beyond utter bewilderment into some vague sense of confidence as a race. "We can handle this!"

Woe and despair have followed as we realize that we have not handled our existence well at all. We remain a crippled animal and we know it. The saddest realization is that we believe that is the best we can do. That despair has been creeping up on us as we try one effort after another (e.g. religion, science, politics, diplomacy, economics) to improve and the woe remains. All of it was built on the sands of the stupour.

We have never, ever thought about humanity itself as the problem *and* the solution. We accept it as just the way it is.

What is wrong with humanity? We have tinkered here and there but never looked at what is wrong with humanity itself. I hope you get it now.

From a tops-down approach, combined human consciousness start with the concepts upon which the overwhelming majority of humanity agree. The one that immediately comes to mind is "we are only human". Which implies that humanity is a mess with nothing to be done. That we are not fit to cope with our capabilities. No question, no detail, just a confusing mess. The various propaganda machines train you to blame it on someone else, anyone else. The finger-pointing is endless.

Almost immediately, after we convince ourselves we are incompetent, it begins to break down into smaller subsegments of humanity. The big two are the right and the left wing perceptions which, in essence, represent authoritarian rule or consensus. Are we just an animal or something more? In the same vein, is brutality or 'love conquers all'.

Can you guess the genders that are behind each? Both are desperate attempts to grasp at straws without meaning.

Break it down further, it begins to resolve into the most ridiculous finger-pointing. There are just a tremendous number of targets to choose from now as the authoritarian points out.

The human consciousness that must be accepted by the vast and overwhelming majority is that we are human, which is so much more than what we are today. Believe it or not, it is something to celebrate, once we fulfill our humanity.

For a human conscious perspective to occur, men must be convinced of their ability to be wholly human. The missing ingredient is men finally convincing themselves that they can perform as a human expects during the act of coitus by transforming it into an expression of their love. They must learn that love and affection are not reserved just for women. That changes the human dynamic irrevocably into something more than an animal's maunderings could ever understand.

Trying to convince all men that they need to *learn* to be human is what has been attempted for three millennia. That is wrong. It could never work. Men need to *learn* to love and share affection openly and *become* human. It won't be the same as a woman's love and affection, of course, but it will be human.

The animal's perspective still remains after all this time. We must capitalize on the gifts that Nature gave humanity. As freaky as it sounds, it seems that Nature really does have a plan.

Men will be kicking the door down to learn how to make coital love once they are *convinced* it is possible. It will be like attempting to stop the tide. The scared little kid grows up.

This is important. Do you get it? We know damn well that men can be good a loving coitus. We have hid from that fact all along because it scared the little boy that he couldn't.

What women know

I was staggered in more ways than one. I have talked before about something I refer to as serendipity. I define this strange version of the word as the perfect timing of an event to fill in the picture, to move one forward, *if one is receptive.*

During this, which I *believe* is my very last book on the subject (we know how that goes), I ran across something that works almost as well as a dialogue would.

Ursula K. Leguin wrote a book, *Words Are My Matter*, in which she has a chapter named "What Women Know".

I won't even try to explain it, except to say that she convinced me, beyond a doubt, that some women have come very close to identifying the problem. That men are the problem. Which is not entirely accurate. It would be more accurate to say that men have a problem with which all of humanity has been complicit.

This great writer got as close as to say, 'the problem is men'. She just could not take that next leap to say why that is true.

The trap

It is surprising and not surprising that she could not make the leap. In my own mind, I believe it is because women have been trained over the millennia to know the truth but leave it suppressed because they could never gather the proof that a man could change his circumstances. There is also the loving sentient nature of the female gender's soft heart.

I think women know, in their heart of hearts what is wrong. Women, in their youth rebel against the restriction in every way they can other than proclaiming what is wrong with men, because they are not certain it can change. Women have enough sense to realize that the proclamation without the realization is a disaster. How could a *woman* prove it? *That* describes better than anything the trap we have been caught in. Men don't want to think about it, women don't want the disaster it would cause to call men out about it, and here we sit. *Kwisatch Haderach.*

The easy route for men is to accept what has been the 'way things are' without change. It makes them lazy. It makes them liars, whether they like it or not. Whether they admit it or not.

The failed act itself makes them takers. The woman's successful act of loving, makes women lovers and givers.

Until men can do the same, we will remain lost.

Altogether, a dialogue would be better and now I know why. Shared consciousness requires it. No more barriers to sharing.

Serendipity

Just to hammer the serendipitous nature of existence home for me, *right* after reading Ms. Leguin's description of the problem, I run across a perfect alternative description that also points to the problem - with a twist.

This one was interesting. I probably won't quote it perfectly, but I will get the essential details right. Pay attention to italics.

Young *men* go to war and kill other young *men* that they don't hate because of old *people* that hate each other but don't kill each other.

It's the "people" that gets me. Along with the previous *men*, it kinda says it all. For some reason, the person that wrote this didn't dare say because old *men* hate each other and don't kill each other. I tried to straighten that out on the site I was visiting.

More exactly, war and conflict is caused by the male. No one has been willing to get to the point. The reason no one has been willing to get to the point is now obvious. I worry, though, that, even though it is obvious to me, you are still scratching your head. Men remained discontented. There's only one reason.

This is another cog in the wheels within wheels. It also points with almost unerring accuracy at the problem. Which makes me wonder if that is why men (especially toxically masculine men) fear women as leaders. Lack of male pride and insanity.

Is it that they fear the woman would not be willing to hate someone with no rational reason to do so? Or, is it a fear that another layer of the sham they have pulled over the human race's eyes will be exposed for all to see? Does it undermine the insane belief that men are leaders for some good reason?

Another interesting point is exposed, also. It is no longer true that it is just men that go to war (though women have been casualties of war since the beginning - often in worse ways than any man). Women now go to war and learn to kill others because we are losing every shred of the sanity we began with as sentient beings so long ago. Even that bastion of women's sanity is wearing away. That is a scary thought.

Bits and pieces

I am having so many breakthroughs and insights that I don't know whether to put them all here. I'll put the most pertinent.

I've often mentioned our topsy-turvy view regarding life. This is *the* example: We make a big deal out of coitus (and sex) in all the wrong ways and suppress the true importance of loving coitus. That must be considered crazy. We can realize the true nature of coitus, which launches loving for a sentient race. All the other ways in which to love one another are not enough on their own. Loving coitus is essential to our sanity.

I always want to add that, if we find it is impossible, that is fine, as long as we face the fact.

I think that is an error. Admitting to the possibility of failure is just wrong. By definitions, a sentient *thinking* race can be masters of our own bodies. The assumption that men may not be able to master their bodies is just wrong. Loving coitus is possible. Any faint thought that it is not is just wrong.

It is just not that difficult. More so, it will get easier as we progress. The first step is overcome the fear of failure.

Snippets & reminders from here and there:

- Our earliest ancestors had not yet developed the powers Nature grants a sentient race in the form of reason and intellect. Instead, through the early availability of imagination and creativity, our ancestors obfuscated and blockaded the attainment of our fully functional sentient state.

- How does a self-aware race treat women equitably while coitus, the foundation of human, sentient existence, and the forge on which the most important human relationship and procreation are wrought, remains inequitable?

- The human desires to please oneself as well as one's mate during coitus. The woman consistently pleases her mate. The man consistently pleases himself during the same act. The two desires seldom merge in both.

The profound effect of a man gaining his pleasure while realizing he failed to please his mate while his mind is on the fritz due to his own orgasm has fractured the male gender's sentient composition. The lack disturbs the mental makeup of both genders, in different ways but, men, by far, the most. I'm not asking you to sympathize. I'm just opening the door for our sentience. We need the lies to end. That's all. It is time for men to step up and make themselves human, once and for all.

The most disastrous disturbance is to the male gender as they continue to fail. Men take, women give, and it begins in bed. It need not remain that way.

- Many of the qualities that we classify as feminine are human, sentient traits that are currently missing, in great part, from the male gender. We only consider them feminine traits because they have yet to reveal themselves in men to any significant degree. Men have been limited by their inability to express their love in its most important form. The form that makes love.

- The male gender is not broken. It is just that those that have experienced the failure for a good portion of their lives become seriously damaged. The male gender's problem is not genetic. It all comes down to post-puberty, for both genders. It can be completely overcome in three generations, if we start today.

And a lot of new snippets:

I hope everyone can see, by now, the complexity of what I am attempting to explain. Three millennia is a long time for humanity to go haywire. We are so far off the beaten path of Nature's intentions for a sentient race that every single aspect of our sentient existence has been distorted beyond recognition. And, yet, the beaten path is still laid out for a sentient race to see.

- Prehumans learn by rote. "Here is what you need to know. Learn it." Humans will learn to think and learn for themselves.

This chapter is bits and pieces that might help explain our predicament or point to elements regarding a human future. The picture of our situation remains hazy because the prehuman has convinced itself that 'perception is reality'. It is not. Not for a human, fully sentient, fully functional human being. A human can distinguish between blatant, self-serving lies and sentient reality. We have a built-in lie detector that is seldom used because it currently out of order.

The image of our completed sentient state is even easier to comprehend because it does not in lying with malicious intent. Malicious lying is a unnatural. A person has to be forced to extremes to spew self-serving lies. It is not human. It is very simple to follow reality when one gender isn't bent on hiding (and hiding from) a single, crucial portion of sentient reality.

The biggest difficulty with this chapter is that the insights are nearly endless. Every aspect of our existence has been bent out of shape by our unwillingness to confront the truth. I have tried to limit the barrage of insights to the ones that seemed most helpful to me or most prevalent in others' minds. That's still a lot.

I am attempting to pack in as many snapshots as possible in this book, glimpses of what has gone on in the past and what might be expect in the future. Often, one may lead to the other.

Realize this is why there are now twelve books. *It's complicated*. As I look back on it, I continued to gather so many more threads in order to assemble the tapestry of our existence, past and future (with a big fat split infinity located right around now - animal to human, sentient, rational, emotionally composed race), which did not completely clarify until this book. That is why we have missed by a mile for three millennia, while strutting around in blind confidence the whole while.

The tremendous, daring, unswerving efforts of the philosophical mind have not been frivolous. The philosopher, throughout the ages, has been chipping away at the falsehood that began long, long ago. They just never got to the right question. What went wrong? Why did we not evolve fully? Or, the way I put it to myself. What is wrong with these people?

As we begin to become human, it will start slowly. A few people will learn to love and see through the stupour that has been in place since the first animal rutted in the woods. It will be an interesting time to be alive. Yes, I know the Chinese proverb. It is why I chose that specific phrase. Keeping our sights on the goal of our humanity may not be easy. Especially for the first few that become fully aware of their humanity as it begins extend itself throughout the whole of the human race. It will be amazing to behold. It will not be as difficult as being the only one around that knows what is going on. Men must finally admit that it is going to take a little effort on the male gender's part to make us human. Just the slightest effort and we are off and running. The benefits are nearly endless. It is a grounds up effort.

Cognitive dissonance & the subconscious

The subconscious contains the unshared thoughts. It is where we hide those pieces of information that are inconsistent with a sentient reality. It contains those pieces of thought that we never want to admit, those pieces of information of which we are ashamed. Those bits of information that are inconsistent with reality cause cognitive dissonance. The biggest of those is the sexual quandary. It pervades the unconscious portion of our race's existence.

Wow! The serendipitous path that led to this. I mean, wow! After the piece directly above, I went on a journey of significance that included a company jerking me around and the paths in my woods.

This all led me to the conclusion that what we have been doing, all along, is distracting ourselves from that which undermines our whole existence.

Which, as I was looking at *Nature*, my next book if I write one, (might be titled, *All The Pieces,* or both), one of the subchapters caught my eye. Cognitive dissonance.

It is what this is all about. There is a cognitive dissonance that was set up three millennia ago, or longer, by the inability of men to satisfy their mate. during coitus. Initially, this turned a lot of men against women (see Plato & Aristotle in the subchapter 'Sappho' below). The double period is because some men have never bothered to find a way to satisfy their mate at all. While others have found a different way. It's all about coitus. At the heart of it all, the unimproved coitus has caused the disturbance to our cognition as a sentient race.

That cognitive dissonance is reinforced every time a man fails to overcome the challenge of loving coitus. It may be less stressful for the man that has found another way but, there remains an undercurrent of frustration. Why can't he last long enough to love a woman the way that nature provided?!!?!

The more I think about it, I think the biggest difficulty is that men are convinced that lasting more than a few seconds is work. They are so wrong, if so. It is just mastery of the male body.

Now, do you see why I consider women special? The are naturally sentient without any real effort. That's not something to be griped about. It was important that one half of the human race was put on the path of sentience. Nature's plan.

I'll go further than that. Maybe what I just said is not exactly accurate. The female is naturally *more* sentient than the male *right now*. The exchange of leadership of the genders in the effort to become more sentient is the norm and ongoing. The more I think about it, the male's mastery of the body is opening a door of incredible potential that leads far beyond loving coitus.

That hit me on another level that I had figured out and mentioned before. Now, it fits even better. Men are hit with the fact that they are disappointing the woman at the most inopportune time. Just as they are experiencing the the most incredible experience of human life, the worst experience of life is occurring. Hence, cognitive dissonance. Every time the man experiences it, his cognitive dissonance drives him crazy and it grows over a lifetime. Let's just say it is difficult to think under such conditions. "I just had the most incredible experience and (mumble, mumble) I didn't last long enough to count.

Which of those two thoughts do you think a man prefers to think about? For too long, men have been given an out. It is reasonable as long as we did not know the answer. Now we do.

The fact that we have avoided reality for three millennia must be accepted. We destroy our sentient reality by not accepting that reality in such spectacular fashion as avoiding the realization that mutual loving is required in its physical form in order to balance out the genders. Because it is possible, the male gender will remain demented or humbled until they learn that they can love in the most Natural manner possible.

The cognitive dissonance destroys the male ego, throws both genders into the grinder of confusion, disabled most of what it means to love, and turns the two genders into armed camps.

It also made it impossible for the male gender to look around and realize that they can learn to love through the act of coitus. They have not been able to confront their need for mastery of their own bodies because we have a three millennia track record that tells them it is impossible. We have never accounted for the effect of cognitive dissonance. We have have had difficulty thinking it through. Loving coitus is dead easy for a sentient race and we know it. Coitus may not be the only way to do so, but it is, by far, the preferred way to do so.

It is just becoming so clear. Women have always had the loving agenda. They had nothing blocking their way except for an insane opposing (not opposite) gender, which shut it all down.

I now wonder whether the subconscious will survive in a human, sentient race. It is the indirect source of emotional instability. The direct source of that instability is rutting coitus. Loving coitus, on the scale of humanity, will eliminate the most destructive content of the subconscious. Is that all that's there?

Sentience

Okay, crazy time. It seems it is the only way to get at what is infuriating me at the moment and explain it well.

Yesterday was one weird day. So many breakthroughs. I guess I'm getting used to it. That's how it happens. I putter around for days, months or, (in the past) years or decades, trying to piece together the insanity that is our current predicament and, then, pieces fall into place like dominoes.

In some ways, it has been like picking up a lot of knotted threads, separating them out, untying the knots, and following each thread to its end in order to tie them together as is required.

One of the rogue thoughts that I just about let run off is the idea of up and coming sentient races. Dogs? Dolphins? Monkeys? Who knows?

At some point, some sentient race seems bound to come along. Some race will breakthrough. Since I have not spent my time figuring out what made us sentient, but was burdened with understanding what destroys our sentient state, I can't make a clue about what it will take for that to happen.

But, what hit me yesterday, is the idea regarding what if another race of beings of a similar sexual conundrum came along? What if a race was guided from the beginning to avoid the horrible experience that humanity has had to endure for the last three millennia? Would it make a difference?

I was of two minds on this. I think the flaw in my thinking had to do with my own long journey through misery. I doubt I can ever straighten myself out completely. There are so many reasons, besides age, that I won't bother getting into it.

If I look at it from that standpoint, the pain I have had to endure along with every other single sentient being on this planet, it seems a horrible burden.

But, then, I think of the young people in the world. Renewal. And I realize it just doesn't matter.

That is the great thing about renewal. In other words, that is the great thing about the cycle of life. The old begrudging, miserable creatures from the past are replaced. Including me.

Will our history of derangement affect us long term? Would a race that is taught to love correctly from the beginning do a better job at sentience? Because of renewal, I doubt it. We should be able to shrug off our three millennium demented state within three generations. Completely.

I am becoming more and more confident about that. Once you get the scent of sentience, it's hard to put away. It's going to be awesome for those that get to live through it. This really makes me root for reincarnation.

I could say that, once we attain our sentient state, it will be okay if we live forever but I seriously doubt that is true. I am beginning to believe we are at the nascent stage of our sentient journey that will be awesome to behold. Loving is just the start of a true sentient existence. Old ideas will always get in the way.

I also believe there will be no desperate desire to live forever, once we attain our sentient state. Loving completes the sentient cycle of life. A full life will be. No need to obsess about living forever because you have never really lived as a sentient being.

There is so much that I am not getting into because it will work itself out, once we become sentient. I am just trying to point us in the right direction in this book.

Right and wrong

Here's another one I've been trying to clarify for ages for you. Free speech versus repression; lies versus suppression.

In the two largest cultural traditions, East and West, the former developed as 'save face' and the latter as lie through your teeth. Both traditions can be traced back to the coital conundrum.

It should be clear to all by now but I feel I should emphasize it. Neither embracing Free Speech nor embracing suppression can ever really work. If you can't look around you at this point in the book, and see that is true, you have had a lobotomy, so I don't feel the need to explain why that is true.

All I really need to say is what I have said before. There are no good solutions until humanity becomes human. Maybe, at this point, you can finally get what I am saying.

I could turn it on its flip-side and say, Free Speech only works once we become human. Or, flip it over-easy by saying suppression is no longer required, once we become human. In either case, it is the retention of the noble qualities with which humanity comes equipped that will make the difference, once it is no longer derailed by confusion and deceit.

It is the same, right on down the line, with every argument regarding the right and the left. They are all half-ass arguments.

There is no good solution to our existence until we become human, sentient, emotionally balanced, self-respectful, loving, and face reality without all of the lies. There is only one (ridiculously simple) way in which we become human.

Alternatives without Resolution

In the absence of the resolution of men's dilemma, the male gender became faced with a matter of accepting two choices.

The resolution of the male conundrum remained untouched *because* of the initial bewilderment and ongoing obfuscation. As I just mentioned above, it seems clear, now, that it is the confounding haywire state of mind created by orgasm coinciding with the devastation of the loving effort (the lack of giving on the part of the man) that did us in for so long.

Make no mistake, resolution itself was rather simple for me to assess. It was just *thinking through* three millennia of nonsense that became the obstacle. The same remains true for the whole of the human race. The complexity of realizing the current situation in toto (e.g. animal instincts) was complicated by the stupour caused by the instincts that developed to hide the issue.

In a simplified manner, men's choices, in the absence of resolution, is to either become docile and humble or revert to the brute tactics of an animal (i.e. male toxicity, the demented state of the male). Neither suits.

In other words, following the woman's gentle lead or dominating through authoritarian procedures defines our current predicament. Both alternatives were chosen by different members of the male gender in varying degrees, mix and match as you please. Neither is a good choice for the male gender or the human race. Men have been caught in the ludicrous trap. This is what maniacs tap into when they spread lies and hate.

I do not discount the female gender's positive influence on our Trajectory. Saying that they saved us from drowning in the stupour is not an understatement.

Women were the sentient anchor that kept us from drifting into the jagged rocks. They kept us from going over the cliff. Without their influence, we would have become extinct or reverted completely to an animal's existence long ago.

They are the ones that held the sentient state's ragged edges together during the millennia of insanity. If you don't think that displays an incredible courage, you are not human yet.

Women's force has been crucial. The female gender's influence is a steadying, stabilizing force rather than a driving force. It is mind-boggling to realize it has held on for three millennia to such a degree. It will remain a crucial force for our sanity, once the opposing force becomes human and no longer an opposing force, but a complementary one.

One sane, emotionally stable gender is not enough.

As I have tried to emphasize throughout the books, the stabilizing force of the female gender *combined* with the driving force of the male gender is the only answer that can ever fulfill the promise of our sentient awareness and intellect. The ramifications of that combined force is almost beyond our imagination and comprehension at this point in time.

I still hesitate to delineate the *sentient* characteristics of the two genders. Stabilizing and driving forces should be close.

It also underlines the reason that loving coitus is so critically important. We cannot attain our sentient state, for so many reasons, without it.   We cannot achieve real equality and equitable treatment of the fairer, stabilizing gender without it.

The forced equality and equitable treatment that we have attempted so far, through legislation and cultural peer pressure, can never suffice. The male gender must fulfill its humanity.

It is nearly impossible to predict how the human male gender will be described. I think 'driving force' will not change but it will not continue to be a mad, obsessive driving force. As I've mentioned a few times, a lot of the characteristics that we portray as female are actually sentient.   Once they begin to appear in men regularly, we will be able to distinguish between the two.

The male's mad and obsessive desire to dominate will disappear once they are convinced their open secret debilitates them. Don't just take my word for it. It is an important stitch in the tapestry that you must see for yourself. Can you begin to correlate all of the bizarre behaviour of the human race, driven by the male gender, due to the desire to hide the ridiculous open secret that is not secret at all?

Maybe to make it more precise, everyone knows (sooner or later) that men are lousy at coitus. It is an open secret, which makes it far worse. The real madness begins with men's desire to quash any spoken thought of it. We let it stay repressed in the subconscious. That describes the insanity fairly precisely.

Wow!   That way of explaining it is important.   It has implications all up and down the chain of history. I could just about write another book just explaining all of the implications. I will probably leave that to a human that has not had the burden of overcoming our prehumanity for a lifetime.

Once the two genders *and* their contributions to conscious awareness are deemed equally important, once we can see the importance of equality and equitable treatment of the female gender, we will be well on our way to move forward into a full display of our sentient prowess. In other words, once unforced equality is attained, our humanity is attained.   We become conclusively human, once and for all. We transcend the animal decisively and without question. There is only one way.

Right now, the male gender's contribution to our conscious awareness remains missing. The female gender's, suppressed.

In brute physical dominance resides the destructive power of the male gender, as it remains in its animal role, to force blindness on itself and the rest of humanity regarding loving coitus as long as the race remains bewildered. I have raised the curtain on that bewilderment and blindness. The animal will continue to hide from it for as long as it can, but conscious awareness cannot be denied forever. It is a part of us, as scary is that may seem. We can overcome it and now is the time.

As I have already said, men can accept nothing less than resolution, which is now available. Even then, it will take convincing before the least human of us will accept it or die off.

The exposure of the lack without full knowledge that it is entirely possible for all men to succeed at loving coitus could never succeed. Just look at the last three millennia.

More so, look at the insane intent to hide from the issue at all costs. Do I need to give specifics? The utter failure and demise of the Free Love generation was for no other reason. They *knew* what was wrong but, without the answer to how men can love, it had to fall apart. (see Feud and the Flower Power generation).

The male gender's physical dominance, which engenders the driving characteristics, makes either of its two fallback choices for dealing with the suppressed conscious awareness damaging.

In the case of reverting to the animal male's position of dominance, they drive us back to the perspective of false and witless surety in order to mask the failure. Might rather than wit. That defines their actions like a cornered animal that accepts delusions, deceit, and surrender to an animal's witless instincts rather than admit they have failed to become human. It, of course, has not been interpreted as such. It is the confidence of a poser, no reality of confidence exists. It is the destructive power of a demented animal. In other words, defeat.

In the case of accepting a humble position, men rescind their driving capacity so necessary for humanity to flourish over the animal perspective and become a dominant, assured, species of sentient life. Self-confidence is wholly missing.

In either case, it is caused by an insidious and defeating elimination of self-respect and self-confidence for men.

Two last points on this subject. The ascension of men into their humanity will be like nothing we have ever seen. Imagine all of mankind finally *really* being confident in itself? I cannot even begin to describe what that will be like. The female's confidence in itself is only compromised by the male insanity.

Secondly, the characteristics of the male gender will change so radically that, again, I cannot begin to describe but I can say this. It will be nothing like the false mask of toxic masculinity or meek acceptance that men wear today. Every single man today wears a mask of some sort, to some extent.

I expect it will continue as a driving force, but one with rationality, sanity, and emotional stability to make it work well.

Some women wear a mask, as well, to 'fit in', but not all. They are not driven to it as men are by the very circumstances of their gender. Women only ply the current game as best they can. The situation leaves some with some portion of their sentience in tact.

Many men wear the toxic caricature, which is the worst of all. Other men do a very good job of adapting to the limited state of their gender. None go without a mask. None helps us attain a fully sentient, rational, loving state.

Men's absent contribution to our sentient state, due to their self-inflicted obfuscation, is the missing element for the full emergence of our conscious awareness. In its absence, men remain the drivers of our madness.

In the presence of their contribution, it will no longer be a matter of misspent driving and stabilizing forces. It will become a mutual effort of two sentient genders working together to make life more meaningful, less conflicted; more human. The human condition becomes balanced. The human state becomes sentient.

The animal will finally be conquered decisively. Dystopia will be put away for good. It won't create utopia but a stable, rational, balanced state of human existence. That seems a certainty. Personally, I think we are launching into an area with no bounds that a prehuman could even begin to imagine.

Three generations

This is certain. Fulfilled love will not be ridden down by all of the nonsensical conditioning we are fed as children, once we gain a foothold in our sentient domain.

All resistance to the nonsense evaporates upon attaining puberty and the utter failure of love. Self-respect gets replaced with doubt. Confidence is shattered. We are more than willing to accept the nonsense as a place to hide from the fearful reality that love is lost for a lifetime.

NO more than three generations, gaining respect and confidence, will be required to end to the wild nonsense that is accepted without question. It may be less.

It will start immediately for those that gain a sentient perspective and slowly filter through to the rest of humanity as they gain theirs. Three generations is more than enough.

Hidden depths

As I put this all together, it becomes clear that while the absence of loving coitus is the source of our problems, it is the way in which we did not deal with it that is the disaster. The blindness and conflict we endorsed in our sentient state is.

The lack of loving coitus left a gap in our conscious awareness, a blank space in our understanding at a crucial and visceral level of our existence. That it has gone on for three millennia as a blindspot without resolution tells the whole story. Our sentient conscious awareness has been intentionally, though inadvertently, overruled by the animal for three thousand years.

We must finally tear down the veil behind which our conscious awareness, as well as our sexual fulfillment and acceptance of our sentient state, has been hidden in anonymity and despair through the ages. It has turned our existence upside down in our desperate attempts to rationalize something that is not rational. Rutting coitus is not for humans. Loving coitus is.

This also explains why I have been so adamant that a few men learning how to love will never do. The resolution has to become part of our shared human conscious awareness, apparent and available to all men. Loving coitus is a sentient trait that must become the common accepted form. Like walking on two legs and talking, it is part of being human.

General guidelines

Everything I have written is meant to explain the incomprehensible gap in our sentient state. I hope I have finally provided it clearly enough for anyone to comprehend and, finally, succeed. There will be no more attempts. I have little doubt that the first minds to absorb the truth will need to be quite perceptive. It is not an easy read, I'm sure. After eleven books, I am rather tentative regarding my ability to penetrate the stupour that is so well ensconced. I've done what I could.

Let me mention a specific bizarre feature of the prehuman condition. It is central to all of our woes and one of our greatest. A great proportion of the misery of our existence is encompassed by the fact that we continue to straddle the animal and human worlds, never fitting into the former or attaining the latter.

There is a paranoia that begins to sit on our shoulder from the time love becomes compromised after puberty, even though we do not recognize it consciously. In essence, that is what begat racism, sexism, misogyny, and all of the other divides that we endure. The animal is still cowering in the corner.

I feel like I am zipping through all of this but, then, I look back at fifteen years and eleven books. If these snippets are not enough. Read the other elven books.

History

As I have said often, I am a polymath. I suck up knowledge like a Hoover sucks up dust (maybe a Dyson is more appropriate nowadays). I seldom delve deeply but scan *everything* I can get my hands on and dive deep when it applies.

I've covered history well, with deep dives into certain periods of interest. Note the quote at the beginning regarding history.

The quote is so appropriate. I have to go even further. History mostly misses the stuff of importance. They concentrate on the wars, destruction, and the who's who of ruthlessness.

History has been most meaningful to me as a vehicle for describing the great swaths of attempts to crack the code on our sentience. It is often well hidden behind the spectacle.

There has been little documentation of our struggle to become human because we have barely comprehended the struggle.

I delved deeply into Ancient Greece because it was the initiation of Western humanity into something resembling coherent thought. How did everything go so wrong? That has been the question I've always asked and the answer I have always been seeking. Everything I found that existed before the flourishing of what is termed Classical Ancient Greece is pretty much gibberish, blathering, or the usual pompous utterances that we still see so often today.

Of course, this excludes the East, which is not because it is not important. While I delved into it, it was not in nearly as much depth. The timing of the rise of coherent thought and the realization of what has been missing seems similar (circa 1st Millennia BCE). I had already become convinced that the issue of our insanity was global. All of humanity is involved, clearly.

The biggest difference between East and West, that I have detected, is the East never seems to have blatantly lied to itself about the subject of coitus. If that is true, it is a big difference. It seems to be reflected in the two attitudes towards life.

Directly preceding the Ancient Greek Classical period was the Ancient Greek Dark Ages, which were preceded by two attempts to achieve humanity. Each fizzled out leading to the Dark Ages.

A much larger story arc that follows the same pattern is the overall human race's development. While there were some bumps and bruises along the way, humanity continued to seek its sanity as it simultaneously strove to excel in a prideful and deluded way for most of the last three millennia.

The more I study history from a different perspective, through actual essays written in different periods, I am pleased to find a few of my summations proved resoundingly accurate.

The story arc of our desire for improvement as a race began to go off the rails completely around the end of the 18th Century.

Our ongoing search for excellence in humanity began to hit a dead end. We gave up. There were lots of long-winded, thoughtful pronouncements in the 18th Century that didn't change a thing. That was our peak. We are seeing the realization of those results, without the fulfillment of loving coitus, in all its misery, disillusionment, aggressive behaviour, and pain, today.

Another confirmation for me was the certainty that nothing we see today is new. The obsessive grasping of many of the wealthy is as old as wealth. All of the arguments about what to do about it are just as old. Neither was a surprise. It is what I realized early on in my journey. All of the superficial issues that do not track to the source of our troubles mean nothing. The troubles we cause will continue on until we become human.

Only loving coitus can make a difference. We will delude ourselves until our noble characteristics naturally come to the fore through the presence of self-respect and self-confidence established by fulfilling our loving nature.

Since the first really coherent thoughts were documented (in my opinion) in Classical Ancient Greece, I peg the beginning of our serious, semi-rational thoughts approximately three millennia ago (in the West). That is also when the first mention of the sexual quandary appears. Before it completely disappeared again for three millennia. Some may argue my example in the West. No one can argue my example from the East.

It must have been such a fascinating time to be alive. Like a baby first opening its eyes to the wonders of the world. The Greeks began struggling with their newly minted awareness provided by the sentient state of existence. They were putting the pieces together for the first time with minimal information and became confounded by the conundrum of coitus.

Pandora's Paradox

Take the story of Pandora's Box (circa 700 BCE) and strip it bare of all of the embellishments of delusions, gods, the accusations of "it's her fault", and other trimmings and you are left with a stunning story that portends our future for millennia. Some ancient humans understood what was missing to some extent. This may very well seem a stretch but I feel certain of it.

The story goes, woman offered a gift to man in the form of a box (which cracks me up). When *man* opened the box, chaos escaped. Hope was left in the box and the lid was closed. It seems clear to me. What else could it possibly be describing?

It is the story of our emergence into sentience and the discrepancy that left us undone as we awakened.

Most simply stated, Pandora's Paradox describes a source of endless complications and trouble arising from a ***single, simple miscalculation*** (from Thought & Co.) and the error of leaving all hope of *remedying the trouble* locked up in a box!

The box is our sentient awareness and the conundrum of the inadequacy of coitus in its animal form that only a sentient race could comprehend. It confounded us and created chaos. It kept us from fulfilling our sentience for three millennia.

The chaos was released (or not resolved) due to the apparent inability to change anything about the situation. The hope that remains in the box *is that someday we* will *overcome the absence of the fulfilling the act of coitus in its human form*.

That is done. It's just a matter of enough men taking the brave initiative to learn how to perform love in the physical manner that Nature provided in order to prove it beyond any doubt.

The chaos will disappear. Hope for humanity will be released.

I am rather convinced that the blame that was laid on Pandora was not part of the original story, but I would have to research a lot further before I could say anything conclusive. In other words, I think it likely that a woman conceived the original story of Pandora's Paradox. A man manipulated it for his own reasons. If you know anything about history, you know that men have been claiming the insights of women for their own all along.

Conceive of some human that realized what a problem humanity faced in the guise of the animal's rendition of coitus and how humanity had already begun to become uncomfortable with the situation that they had begun to sense (this is certain: it was first sensed and articulated during this period of time).

A sensitive person, before all of the walls were erected to avoid thoughts on the matter, would not have had a difficult time seeing what was going on. Sappho seems a possibility, even though the timeline doesn't line up well. As bisexual, she would know the benefits of mutual satisfaction and the detriments of men's situation. She was also very outspoken and insightful.

A smart person could have easily extrapolated the conflict it would cause and, further, realized that humanity would be able to cope with it, sooner or later, (make coitus a loving event) once humanity had matured and gained critical knowledge.

The only thing such a person could do was compose a story like Pandora's Paradox in an attempt to warn humanity. "Don't lose hope! We'll figure it out, sooner or later! Don't hide the problem away. *That* would be the real disaster." I could have told her it would never work.

There is evidence that the original story predates Hesiod's version. Evidence also implies that the original story *did not* implicate the 'first woman' (in this case, Pandora) with being at fault. Considering it is only a very small piece of the puzzle of our lost humanity and it is well obscured by the millennia, I have not pursued further yet. I had just always been puzzled by this myth and its misconstruction in The Garden of Eden.

Women were eventually blamed for all of our ills. What would cause men to blame women? Only one craven reason fits all of the facts. Men were looking for a scapegoat.

The Kama Sutra

The *Kama Sutra* (circa 400 BCE), in another part of the world, was not too much later in time and it addressed the exact same issue in a different way. In India, at least, and seemingly the only place in the world, men attempted to struggle with the problem rather than just bury it. They had some sense.

Kudos to that author, though. I mean, damn! That was a good try, though it could never work on a human-wide scale. It could never become adopted by all of humanity. It was way too complicated. But, that he even tried says a lot about the culture.

The *Kama Sutra* further confirmed, inaccurately, what everyone already erroneously believed. That there was a time limitation attached to men's performance. The best that could be done was make it complicated. Wrong but good try!

More importantly, it confirms beyond the shadow of a doubt that awareness of the issue dates dates back three millennia.

Pandora's Paradox was the first warning. The *Kama Sutra* was the first published attempt to do something about it.

The Garden of Eden was one of the first nails in the coffin regarding any discussion or any further thinking on the matter in the West and introduced the big lie.

A summary of the Garden of Eden: Knowledge is a curse, thus our sentience is cursed. Wail until the roof collapses. Make stuff up rather waiting for the truth to become evident.

Can you guess what knowledge was cursed? Since right down through the ages, the same religion has also cursed sex, it is straightforward. The church's declaration that sex was only good for making babies, the same. The curse on any alternatives, the same. It is the blind forcing their blindness on others. It was one of the first, most extensive coverups of the subject of all time.

The snake cracks me up every time. Almost as much as the christian idea of the "Second Coming", which always has me rolling in the aisles. If you think about the latter in the context of what I am explaining, it is truly hilarious.

I respect Vatsyayana's book (the author of *Kama Sutra*) and India because he, due to the culture in which he lived, at least made the attempt to make coitus a loving act, even though it was way too complicated to resolve anything. No other culture on Earth ever even made such an attempt or faced the issue at all.

The issue with coitus is not complicated. It only *seemed* complicated. It was conditioned into us to believe there was nothing to be done as it was *very* simple minds that initially attempted to see beyond their capabilities to comprehend.

Vatsyayana Mallanaga even admitted as much. He stated that he had studied earlier masters in his quest to improve sex (shades of three millennia of conditioning). The same condition can be said to apply to all of humanity for the last three millennia.

All down through history, men have believed that they are on a time limit as soon as they penetrate because that is what they were told and that is how it works for animals. They could not delve deep enough, because of the conditioning, to realize that there were fundamental flaws in the original conclusions.

The logic has been: it is true of the animal, therefore, it is true of a human. We have never taken our sentience into account.

Mallanaga was programmed to fail, like all of humanity since.

A human isn't destined to fail at loving coitus. If he uses his brain for other than decoration.

Sappho

Sappho (600's BCE) Note the time discrepancy I mentioned. Dating seems vague enough to allow for Sappho to have written Pandora's box. The more I read about Sappho, the more realistic it becomes that she wrote Pandora's Box.

While it may be a stretch to say she wrote Pandora's Box, it is certain she turned the male world upside down. She made it very clear that women can fully share in the sexual pleasure, just as much as any man. This shook the world. It may be the single most significant difference between the Western world and East.

While she has been studied more than just about any other woman, her radical views made her someone that many men were very happy to disenfranchise. Like many of the written works of that time, Sappho's were destroyed. The madmen of the time decided to destroy knowledge. It's not even surprising. There is reason to believe her work was intentionally destroyed.

She was an extremely insightful poet. It fits the bill. I won't claim it to be a certainty. Almost anything written about Sappho, other than her name, is not certain but vague innuendoes.

Sappho may have had the fullest expressed comprehension of the importance of the physical aspect of love ever. She existed before the whole discussion was shut down with prejudice. Of course, she understood. As a bisexual, she knew what it means to *share* love and made no bones about it. She could probably see clearly how destructive it was for a man to fail, since she saw it before it was covered up and hidden away behind the stupour. She was not particularly popular.

To make the timeline of Pandora's paradox more complicated, I ran across information that suggests that even Pandora's Box had a precedent in Sumeria. It's just too far back in time to verify much of anything. As it is all little more than an anecdote, I did not see the purpose in further study. The evidence of the failure of prehumanity is very clear in so many other aspects.

She almost certainly was the first woman to express the many aspects of love, including the physical aspect that she could only find with another female. Her writings were suppressed with a will over the next millennia as men's failure became more apparent. This is why I tend to believe that she might have written Pandora's Box. No man would have written it.

Another point is very clear. Misogyny was already present by the 1st Millennium BCE. Plato and his sidekick Aristotle both voiced the opinion that women were lesser beings. Note also that these two had a great disdain for coitus. They were not too fond of Sappho, either, nor her lesbian leanings. It all fits.

Sex, at that time, for men, was anything goes. Women, not so much. Sound familiar? Men posturing and doing as they please but never talking about it is the theme of prehumanity.

Misogyny may be a poor word for the actual situation. It was suppression of women, pure and simple.   Part of that was misogyny but it comprised far more than that. It still does.

Sappho was also smart enough to realize that the physical aspect of love was not everything. It was just one component of love. The other two she termed, beauty and goodness. But, she *knew* how important the physical component of love is. It just stuns me that someone (and I do not find it surprising that it was a woman) understood all of this so very long ago.

This is important and I may not have stressed it enough through the books. Loving coitus just opens the door for all of the myriad forms of love to flourish. Sappho was a stunning woman. She spoke so much truth, before the truth was shattered.

Once the male gender is no longer impeded regarding the considerations of love, love can flourish in all of its many forms, including maybe the next most important form.

That form is not the love of one's fellow human but the more sophisticated, *sentient* concept of love of the human race, humanity itself. All of it.

The untarnished human being's efforts are directed towards fulfillment of the human *race*.   *Not* individual aggrandizement. Nothing less suits a sentient race. Nothing near that insight can be expected from animals or prehumans.

The many aspects of love

For the sake of the love in an intimate relationship, I particularly like Gary Chapman's *Five Languages Of Love*.   It addresses what I have heard so often from women.   "It's really affection that counts". In other words, the other ways that love is expressed between a couple. In the absence of loving coitus, it is only a stopgap. In its presence, love will flourish.

A man cannot feel honest in his affection for a woman when he causes the physical act of love to utterly fail. A promise that he fully expected to fulfill up until he reached puberty and it all begins to fall apart. Many feel that the love story is a sham. That is not the case. Only the prehuman enactment has been a debacle.

A man feels like he has betrayed his lover, and been betrayed by life as well, before he ever gets started on truly expressing his love. Can you imagine the head spin that causes for the rest of his life? If you are a man, you don't need to imagine.

It seems certain that the more abstract descriptions of love were created after the damage to the concept of physical love became evident. As the absence of achieving loving coitus left only despair and bewilderment, some abstract concepts were created to fill the gap. In other words, we gave up and changed the story. It's never been a good story. It's been another lie.

"Waitaminute, we didn't really mean physical love! Just sticking it in is close enough. No, love is this ephemeral concept for the purpose of getting women in bed and writing poetry."

It has taken us three millennia since our first emergence into a sentient state to open our eyes, while our sentient faculties remained in disorder, but I have finally opened the damned box and released the hope.

Not that anyone's been listening. Sometimes, I picture people singing la-dee-da, la-dee-da loudly to themselves, with their hands over their ears while I shout it out.

We can be human. We can learn to love as humanity deserves and of which humans are fully capable, in the way that Nature provided, with the tools Nature granted humanity! We are not human and sentient until we can succeed at loving in the most natural manner possible.

Nobody has been listening.

(just a little hyperventilation)

Freud and the Flower Power generation

Maybe the first big break in the sexual confusion was Freud. He was the first to put sex on the map. All of the quirks of our sexual drama were first exposed and studied openly by Freud.

Even so, Freud could not comprehend that the repression of sex is a sign of why the whole human race is unhinged. He attempted (like most everyone throughout history) to pin the blame for any problems on individual quirks or psychological trauma, rather than the whole prehuman condition. It was just another act of desperation to avoid the single most crucial issue at all costs. Irony in spades.

There is an example of the irony of our sexual dilemma, due to a number of factors, that emphasizes the incredibly strange situation. Men love sex. Men have also been in charge for so long it's almost impossible to find a time or location where they weren't (okay, Lesbos, three millennia ago).

So, why in the world would the topic of sex be repressed if men dominate? There's only one answer. Sex presented an issue that men could not confront without resolution being already available, but they still wanted sex. Their shame is written all over the enforced blindness of the situation.

They don't want to talk about their failure. They just want to get their rocks off and forget about it by morning. Forget all of the complications. The woman might as well be a sock.

They buried it with a mad and witless will. The need for babies made it easy to do. It was about survival of the species.

Another of the ironic aspects is the combination of the repression of the subject of sex while, simultaneously, it remained seemingly unapparent to men that the problem is rampant among men. Too many men clearly take it as a personal affront and clearly question how many other men suffer, if any. Only of late were men assured that they are all lousy at coitus. Sadly rather than put it all together, they accepted the conclusion.

The unhinged state is reflected in so many aspects of human life, but most directly, in misogyny and its counterpart, the toxic masculine mask that many men wear; the facade they have been carrying around with them always to counter the fact that they never wanted to admit. It is the chip on many men's shoulder.

Can you see the problem with legislating misogyny out of existence? It can't happen. The micro-aggressions and bad feelings, at least, will remain as long as coitus remains stunted.

It has taken many generations since Freud just to ask the question why the *human race* represses sex?

The repression of the topic of sex, along with misogyny and the toxic masculine mask, are not aspects of just a few individuals, cultures, or belief systems. They are global phenomena that spans all cultures and all boundaries.

Freud attempted to target quirks and perversions of individuals rather than the prehuman condition. Humanity was not ready to accept that it is a phenomenon that can only be addressed by humanity as a whole, and the male gender in particular.

The Flower Power generation addressed the repression with a bang and came so achingly close to the critical breakthrough.

Unfortunately, they fell victim, naturally enough, to the garble that humanity has made of it since forever. It is a circuitous route. How does one open themselves to the possibility that coitus can be more without breaking down the walls of repression? How does one break down the walls of repression without realizing that coitus can be more? It took me a lifetime. Without the Flower Power generation breaking down the walls, I don't believe I could have taken the next step.

Note that the Flower Power movement was mostly comprised of children just reaching the age of puberty and the desire for fulfillment. They had been fed a story and they wanted to make it true. Little did they know, that was not the full story. They sensed that there was a problem and they were outraged. How could adults leave them to be so blindsided??!!?!

Because we have always misconstrued the situation, it is no surprise that they did not succeed in overturning the debacle. The bewilderment remained and still does.

They did not get an answer or even formulate the problem well. They couldn't pin it down. Something was wrong and they damn well knew it. That was enough. They hated the situation but, just like every generation before them, they were slowly assimilated into the nonsense. Kudos for even attempting to address it, before they fell victim to the droning inertia of "that's just the way it is" but the inertia finally had its way with them.

Even though they used the right words, the Flower Power Generation missed by a mile. They said the words but did not really understand the deeper meaning behind the words, "Free love." All they got was free sex.

The Flower Power generation connected all of the right dots; love, sex, humanity, and the finer qualities of the human race; but still they couldn't quite put their finger on it. They felt the pulse but never touched the heart of the matter.

To get so close and still miss the mark is noteworthy. It is on the tip of everyone's tongue (no pun intended) of late and, yet, we could never quite find the words to express the reality, even when *everything* was right there in front of us! Twelve books tells the story of how difficult it has been for me.

The proposal of 'Free Love' rebelled against the repression of the topic of sexuality, but went no further. Another crucial milestone, but not the last and, certainly, not enough.

Another generation conceded defeat to the beast in sheer consternation. It was a huge step forward but something remained missing. The beast won, again.

That generation created the important milestone of freeing humanity from its forced blindness regarding sex but, still, it gave no real answers and created further delusions and confusion. Even with all of the obvious counterpoints since, we still avoid admitting that coitus can be so much more. The boulder keeps rolling over everything in its path.

Do you see where it has always fallen short? How brilliantly the barrier was erected? The barrier was erected to avoid the topic of sex, not just coitus. Thus, it blockaded any discussions on coitus through many previous layers.

Even the Flower Power generation only got as far as exposing the topic of sex. They did not even come close to exposing the lack in coitus. Instead, they freed the whirlwind of alternatives. If coitus can't make love, there are other ways.

It is truly a conundrum wrapped in an enigma, blurred beyond recognition, and baked for millennia.

Another striking aspect in the development of our awareness of the situation just hit me. I have wondered for a long time why it all broke open with the Flower Power or Free Love generation.

I mention often the fact that a vague sense of what was wrong hit with fury during the 1960's. Something had opened our eyes. Something made us aware of the shameful state we had been living, even though, now, less than one hundred years later, once again, it has been hushed up, scuttled, placed in limbo.

The world fell in love with the love story. The first one was written in the mid 18th century. Romance novels and movies became a big thing since that time. It rode too close to the taboo subject. Bang. That was the trigger that took two centuries to finally fire. All hell broke loose for a generation.

(an aside: read the book written by William Goldman and titled *The Princess Bride: S. Morgensterns's Classic Tale of True*

Love and High Adventure; he dared to go beyond the 'happily ever after' and drilled into the reality of a prehuman existence and what really happens after happily-ever- after is demolished. it is so refreshing to hear the truth of the real prehuman state).

The stunning point is that, as love stories developed, the physical component of love could not be avoided or ignored. It slowly became part of the love story. It had to be addressed. In addressing it as vaguely as possible, all of those prepubescent expectations of love, boiling with hormones, hit like a hurricane and, finally blew it all sky high. It is just more evidence that everyone knows intuitively that there should be more to coitus.

People read or watch movies about how wonderful love is, which, when a person is exploding with hormones, means one thing, coitus. They proceed to the actual joyous event only to be totally disappointed and blindsided by the failure.

The distractions, delusions, the bluff and the scam have continued to become much more sophisticated over three millennia to keep pace with our conscious awareness.

If I had not been willing to completely step away from the nonsense we endure on a daily, almost moment by moment basis, I could have never gotten to the final answer.

The Flower Power generation deserves a place in history because they did not just open the door. They did not just knocked it down. They blew it apart. They came so achingly close to revealing what is wrong with mankind. They were a key player in the fight for our humanity and love.

"Free Love" says it all and we still missed it. Just as "Make Love" says it all and we purposely misinterpret its connotations, much less its precise wording. Two words say it all! **"Make** love"! The Flower Power generation was a generation that adamantly rebelled in full regalia against the fiasco of our failed sentient state. They came so very close (pun intended).

They broke the layer of the taboo that kept us from examining anything regarding the subject of sex. One more layer was left.

An interesting human potential is held within the eye to eye penetrative sexual intercourse, called coitus, that humanity does naturally. There is only one other animal that engages face to face and, of course, they are not fully sentient and never even consider sharing the pleasure fully. *They are just an animal.*

We are the only species that can *consciously* look into the eyes of our partner during coitus with the *expectation* of fulfillment and make it so. Yet, the desire remains to turn the lights out, because we have never made it so.

Now you know why. The expectations are seldom achieved. The anticipation makes it a ship wreck. We have always realized something was missing from coitus. We just turned away.

The tendency to turn out the lights is reminiscent of misogyny and the repression of sex. It presages the real problem and *all* of the quirks that we have gone to ridiculous lengths to suppress.

Freud was both right and wrong. He was right because it *is* all about sex. He was wrong because once we achieve loving coitus, it will *no longer be* all about sex.

We will be ready to call ourselves human. The obsessive, destructive fascination with sex and violence is because of the ongoing failure. It will no longer remain obsessive as it becomes loving. As it becomes fulfilling, the obsessions go away. The madness goes away.

No dissatisfaction or obsession remains when the act is fulfilled. Love takes its place; we become human and emotionally stable.

Renewal

As I finally, after eleven books, get over my outrage that it took humanity more than three millennia to realize what it means to be human (as well as me being stuck with the bill), I begin to see why it makes so much sense.

Actually, by any other measure except a single lifetime, like a geological age, or even the age of the human branch of life, the three millennia it has taken is but an instant.

The short lifespan of humans (~40 years) before today, contributed to understanding and resolution taking so long. People were scrabbling to get by until the day they died. No one had the luxury of sitting back, much less completely exiting the prehuman condition (as I had to do), in order to think things through. The mid-life crisis was nonexistent. It wasn't mid-life. It was death. Still, my route has been arduous.

There is also the curious way in which life proceeds on an individual basis. We come into the world full of vigour and not a single thought in our heads. We are ready to be amazed. Life seems an amazing mystery to explore, savour, and enjoy.

We proceed into life with the highest expectations and have a difficult time admitting at pubescence that something is off. Worse yet, the previous generation is more than willing to assure us that we are 'just maturing'. Nose to the grindstone. Right.

The mystery turns into misery.

Call it the exuberance of youth or high hopes. We go forward into life with a will, little sense, and the highest anticipation. We get clobbered from behind without the slightest realization because of the conditioned blindness fed to us in our earliest days. We try to shrug it off. It takes a toll on all. More importantly, and the reason I drove forward on this path throughout my lifetime, it takes a deadly toll on the human race.

We're told that we are just 'maturing'. We are told that the innocence of youth is just a childish dream we need to get over. (can you feel me beginning to hyperventilate?)

Over and over again, through the millennia, the youth has cried for surcease. "Something is wrong, dammit!" "No, no, child. Life is misery. Just accept that fact." We succumb, once again, to the inertia of history, the past, and the stupour as puberty, disillusionment, and failure take hold. We are welcomed into the fold of misery with open arms.

I've often discussed 'the mid-life crisis' in previous books. It seems clear that what is missing from life creeps up on us over a lifetime and blindsides us, even though we have experienced the failure over and over, again, throughout our lives.

It is the reason we see, right now, today, so many old pompous men trying to recover their balance by following the village idiot.

The shock of the overwhelming sensual, sexual experience wipes the mind clean for the male each time or, at least shunts aside any suspicion that all is not right. This may get to the actual crux of why it has taken three millennia. The disparity between the mind-washing joy of the experience and the awful realization that something is horribly wrong have a difficult time coexisting. "Difficult" is an understatement since it has taken three millennia for it to finally come home to roost.

Worse yet, the failure causes many men to attempt to justify the situation that they fear and don't understand at all. That they can't confront in any manner. This is that which creates all of the irrational thoughts and behaviour.

The bliss the man experiences overrides the uncomfortable feeling that something is seriously wrong. That is the stupour. All of the behaviour of those in the throes of a mid-life crisis are dead giveaways. They are seeking that which has always been missing since their youth. As their life nears its end and the flame begins to go out, desperation sets in and the subconscious awareness begins to make itself felt.

Here we sit, three millennia later.

Varying aspects

There are so many aspects of this that I fear will be questioned and I am doing my best in this one book to cover as many as possible, since I know very well now just how comfortable humanity is in its stupour, even as the world literally burns.

I have highlighted some, that are repeated in the other books, because they seem so close to the surface of the stupour. Many that are in the other books will just have to remain there.

This is one that has continued to bother me. "Well, what if I don't want to engage in coitus? What if I prefer my sexual pleasure in some other form?"(or, not at all). I expect, though I could be wrong, this statement would only come from a woman.

There are valid reasons that a woman may rather not engage in coitus or not experience sex or orgasm in any form (though the latter seems unlikely). It might 1) make her pregnant or 2) force her to take a disagreeable pill in order to feel mostly safe from pregnancy, 3) or, maybe, I don't know, but there are probably others. One, in today's world is very clear. Men's behaviour repels them. The worst, of course, is if she is just conditioned so.

The last is another quandary. Many women are repelled by the awful behaviour of men and rebel against it. What concerns me is that many cannot even conceive of the idea that the male gender's behaviour can change. I have discussed this with some. They cannot believe men can learn to love and be human. This is reasonable in the context of the stupour but concerns me.

The invalid reason that is most prevalent today, though, is that women don't get pleasure from coitus or, its counterpart, the lack of affection on the part of a male. That is the flip-side of the misery of humanity that led to so many wrong conclusions.

It is the same answer as what I said regarding not everyone having the chance to enjoy the splendour.

It is *not* that everyone *has* to engage in the most loving act in existence. It is that men *have* to have their humanity (*not* their masculinity) confirmed. They have to know, as a gender, that they are no longer just an animal. It is that tension that half of the human race brings to our affairs in the absence of loving coitus that is the problem. It requires an effort that the male gender has not yet faced. Humanity must know that, if they *do* engage in coitus, it *will* be the splendid act that humanity has always *expected*. This is crucial to men's resultant sanity.

Alternatives are fine as long as both agree to them. I expect, if they don't agree, they will go their separate ways. It may become one of the first topics of discussion for potential lovers. That is, once sex and coitus become open topics for discussion.

Most importantly, it is necessary that men *know* that they will not fail at the act at which, as they remain an animal, they have failed throughout history. It impedes their ... wholeness? (I get tired of repeating 'their self-respect and self-confidence, which impedes their nobler tendencies and humanity', but, yeah, that).

Noble characteristics

It mystifies me to realize that we have known all of it all along. I have zero doubt, as I continue to study more deeply and confront the stupour with more clarity.

It is everywhere to be seen. It begins with the noble characteristics. We have known the noble, honourable characteristics all along. I should probably provide the full list of noble characteristics (it's in other books) but I don't see the point. I should probably be bitter at this point, but I'm not. I'm just exhausted and disappointed. It is all there for anyone to see. It may be one of the most fascinating aspects of all of this as I break through the barrier.

It is there, right in front of each and everyone of us and, yet, we can't see. I also become more and more mystified by the fact that I could see through it. Out of tens of billions of people over the millennia, how did it come down to me?

Maybe it is just a matter of this that I am currently experiencing. The truth, the clarity, is just awe-inspiring.

The noble characteristics are built in. It is part of sentient consciousness and clarity. Please excuse that I use sentient awareness and conscious awareness interchangeably. They are one and the same. I think sentient consciousness connotes the nature of the gift that Nature provided far better and its effect on humanity. Sentient consciousness makes all of the noble characteristics the natural result of attaining our humanity.

The noble characteristics are decimated as each life progresses. The growing lack of self-respect and self-confidence in a man decimates all. Just look at the best of women, if you have any questions.

I reiterate what I said earlier. We *unlearn* how to be human.

By the way, as I was just rereading *Sentience*, I really like the list of questions that I assembled over a lifetime that needed answering, even though it has taken twelve books to answer some coherently to the slightest degree. It should help explain.

Unique in our affairs

The male gender's dilemma, once overcome, holds tremendous promise. Only the male gender is required to prove its sentience, its humanity, by overcoming this hurdle set by our animal past. Once it is done, the male gender will prove more beneficial than just the absence of the brute animal's presence in our affairs. I can't quite put my finger on all of it, but it is certain. We have big lovely surprises ahead of us.

The Broken Cage

Something else has been niggling at the back of my brain for a long time, but I could never before quite make enough connections, until now, to articulate what had been bothering me in a semi-coherent manner. It has to do with the effect of all of this on the female gender. The thoughts are still quite remedial, but I will explain it as best I can. I guess, in general, what I get out of it is, once again, what an awful confusion lies between the animal state and the human state. I know, in this lifetime, I will only be scratching the surface, no matter how hard I try.

It will take the effort of a fully formed human race to really, finally, get to the bottom of it all. The revelations will just keep coming for quite awhile yet. They will look in the rear-view mirror, which will help a lot in explaining the confusion.

Don't take what I say here as anything more than a first attempt to illustrate a fundamental change in our circumstances once we become sentient. That is, this has not been rigorously reasoned out yet. The basic elements should hold, though.

The effect of our stunted humanity on women has been difficult for me to query and put into words. I don't mean the brutal way the prehuman male has treated them. That *should* be obvious to everyone before they ever pick up this book. Anyone with a brain should already be well aware of that heinous, most disruptive aspects of the situation. This is more subtle.

From our disruptive beginning, all of the awful effects of the male gender have been spawned. This addresses more subtle aspects of the past and future relationship nuances.

I now have at least a piece of it as I pulled on a corner of the tapestry. The whole effort of peering into a sentient future, is more of an effort than assembling a rational perspective of our past - and that took me twelve years. This is my first foray into assembling something resembling a scenario planning effort to extrapolate what a fully capable sentient future might look like.

This is only one of those pieces. It begins to drop a lot of pieces into place. I am considering another book, if I am not, once again, utterly disappointed with the acceptance of this.

Unfortunately, I don't like the way this is described but I don't know how else to convey it at this time.

As I think in this context, it becomes clear than an essential component of any life form's existence is missing from Maslow's chart. Coitus/sex. Maybe it is considered an element that is, by necessity, always in place. While true, *loving* coitus is not. It should be there, as I've already explained. It is *not* in place and it is essential to our humanity. It is the *most* important aspect of the chart for a sentient race and it is missing. No surprise there.

The female has been trained to attract mindless men because, especially when it comes to sex and women, men are altogether pretty mindless. That may show the true humanity of the female gender best. Let me try to break that down for you.

All life is born to procreate. While, like most of Nature's intentions we have overturned that apple cart, there is still a strong desire to make babies. So, by that rule of thumb, women attempt to rationalize finding some form of man that is a little better than scrapings off the bathroom floor. So far, there has really only been one attractant for men. Just like an animal.

Worse yet, many men are repelled by women being more than sex objects because that is, sadly, all the prehuman male, so much closer to an animal, wants or needs, or can tolerate. Few can handle more. The closer to an animal, the more this is true. Men have been trained only to take.

Since I am not a woman, I have to guess what is going on. We talk about the "genetic desire" to make babies. I am not so sure. That is not the way I read what I hear from women. I think it is a *sentient desire* to make babies that keeps women going. Which makes the woman's part in things even more remarkable. It is heroic that they are willing to tolerate so much they *know* is coming at them once they commit to having a baby with some barely human cretin. All for the sake of carrying on the species.

In that context, I am utterly and irrevocably staggered.

Women have learned to doll themselves up to be attractive to the male prehuman animal. It is all that is require and, in most cases, all that is desired. The only thing that will attract many men is blatant, irrefutable sexuality (just check the offensively titillating ads on the web that cry out to the basest nature of prehumanity and the unfulfilled act of coitus in order to get click. since they fill the web pages, they must be quite lucrative).

This reminds me of a time when I went somewhere far away from much of civilization for many years, at a time when the Flower Power generation was fairly dominant, and makeup was virtually nonexistent. When I returned, most women had all of this goop on their faces. I was appalled. I never got used to it.

I am not suggesting that women (nor men) will lose all desire to be attractive, once men can finally and consistently love women for their many other attributes. It is just that the attractiveness of both will adapt to a sane representation of the two genders that indicates far more than the desire to have sex.

Think about how this works out. A man, somewhere deep inside, knows he has little to offer when it comes to the most essential act of life. He is desperate to find a woman, but knows he is lacking. At this point, any woman will do. He can't be choosy because he knows he is a failure. Any woman that looks his way and displays a desire for sex will do. He'll be thankful.

I know how difficult this will be for many to accept because of the blur we have put on relationships. All of the male 'attractants', like money, power, fame, etc are just a substitute of the real thing. Does that help?

This should be going off like a blinding flare for you as far as how much the human condition will change due to this one factor. Money, power, fame, and all of the ludicrous desires that bend the human condition completely out of its true shape will no longer be important on the insane scale that is desired today. Yes, folks will desire to be successful but for totally different reasons than a witless animal could ever conceive.

When equality finally kicks in. Both genders will be signaling the far more complex indication of their desire for a suitable companion, lover, friend, and life partner. Today, often, men are only interested in is getting laid. Just like an animal.

In other words, a big part of the transformation of our existence is women finally come into their own. Equality actually existing and, men not being obsessed about getting laid.

Once men have confidence in themselves as lovers, the whole game changes. Sex becomes a secondary concern. Men will seek more than just getting laid from a woman, once they know they are competent at loving. They will be more interested in expressing love in the only manner it is possible. As a human.

I think the paint and all of the games I have always despised will fade away in very short order. Men will learn that there is far more to women than just satisfying *their* sexual needs. As I try to state often, the obsessions of humanity will cease to be.

In fact, by necessity, as the situation evolves, men will desire far more from women than just red lipstick and a sexy walk as their minds are freed from the insidious delusions of the animal and the desperate desire to find some woman that will tolerate the lousy sex, which is all he has to offer.

This is also why men posture.

The war paint, and male gender's preposterous displays of manliness, will evolve into something human. In other words, sexual attraction has been perverted by our perverted and distorted view of existence. It is the same reason that porn, perversions, and obsessions exist: the stupour.

Here is another point that I doubt many have ever considered. Men purposely made women dependent on them. To some extent, it may have been part of the program of evolution; children, etc. There is evidence, though, that suggests that is not the case. The animal that man remains, mostly, has one desire from women: get laid. Men are so terrible at it, of course, they developed a system that forced women to be dependent. I have met so many women that were doing nothing more than looking for some man to lay their claim, so that they could survive with a little shred of respect and ease. It breaks my heart every time.

It will be a step by step process as the man slowly awakens from his mindless vacuum toward the finer aspects of a human existence and women respond by developing all that has been stunted by their precarious position of the past.

Gosh, now I really wish I could stick around for another hundred years to watch this slow, stunning transformation take place as women finally reveal themselves to humanity. 'Dazzling' doesn't even begin to express. Because I am not female, I always have difficulty trying to describe their dilemma.

Achieving true success

We can begin the transformation into a race of competent, sane sentient beings right now. *Right now.* You must first realize and accept that the current human condition is nothing other than insane, just as it has been since our first consciously aware sentient thoughts on love and coitus drove us beyond our available comprehension. Nature had provided the tools for which we had not yet developed the comprehension to utilize. We stuck the thoughts in a back corner and forgot all about them.

Within two or three generations, we can fulfill our sentience to the extent that we know full well how to love, gain our sentient self-respect and confidence as individuals and a sentient race, and begin displaying our noble human qualities consistently.

What surprises me is when I am accosted with such comments as "humanity's plate is too full right now" to be contemplating how to become human. ??!?!?!?! I could not believe it when I read that. We would prefer to proceed with our destruction?

Do you think that it's new that humanity has a lot on its plate? The 'plate' is full due to the same distractions that men have used to delay the inevitable for three millennia because they are scared to death that their failure would be exposed with no recourse. That there is recourse is what this is all about.

I guess I'm just ranting. The person did say they would see what else I had to say. TWELVE books!?!? Who's listening?

I hear people saying how they are fighting for humanity (both left and right political viewpoints believe this) and, yet, they are not changing a damned thing of import over the long haul. They are living the day-to-day of the animal. I am living the eternity.

Every day, we will continue to face unbounded nonsense until we become human and truly understand the profound concepts of sentience and love. The right and left, and all the other labels, have been fighting forever ... over nothing of import in the grand scheme of things. They are picking away at the scabs of the prehuman state and making us bleed, over and over and over.

Once in a great while, it might be nudged a little in a better (or worse) direction. The distractions and superficial issues are like a revolving door that the prehuman race has never exited.

As long as we don't grasps the truth of our humanity, we fail. One argument of the prehuman is just as strong as any other because they are all so full of holes.

What is just so sad to contemplate is all of those, now and in the past, that have groveled and fought over meaningless scraps thinking they were getting the best life had to offer. How sad.

The Long, Grueling Journey

It is rather fascinating the steps that I had to take to get here.

The Trajectory of Life is one, rather new, cornerstone of my work. Humanity is the only projection along the newly extended Trajectory of Life on Earth to date.

The new trajectory that sentience ensures is just starting. Conscious awareness is the first extension along that trajectory. It liberates us from the narrow and random vectors of genetics and sets aside the witless instincts of the animal to provide a new form of improvement for a species.

The first step in moving that trajectory forward was a race of beings rising above all others to rule (shades of Maslow's Hierarchy). That happened not so long ago. As the leading race of beings on this planet, we should be stewarding the planet and all of its life forward. We aren't because we have not got over ourselves. We have remained befuddled by our potential for so much more than we ever suspected and have mostly created destruction in the wake of our ongoing stupour.

Our coincident stewardship has been missing in action. We have been so involved with the manic mania, struggling with the confusion implied by our emergence into our prehumanity (generally, that is displayed as two viewpoints fighting each other to the death; over and over and over again throughout history; same subject, new decade). We have spent no time improving the conditions for Nature and/or Humanity in any significant way. Instead, we have been wrecking everything.

The trivial toys we produce are just that. Trivial toys. We whine about what we would do without our toys that are destroying all of life on Earth.

We have never been willing to look in the mirror and admit that something is wrong with humanity that must be addressed. The accoutrements of sentience don't yet fit.

We have never spent a second improving humanity itself in any meaningful way. Just like coitus (and because of the sexual debacle), we avoid the issue entirely. We throw up our hands.

Psychiatry, sociology, psychology, and philosophy have all been sidelined by the great distraction. In every case, rather than admit that there is something wrong with humanity itself, we always try to pin it on individuals that are nothing more than victims of the circumstances of our inability to become wholly human. Maybe the scope of the real problem was just too vast, too complex for anyone before to attempt to correlate it all.

It was not easy. Hence, twelve books. It took a level of dedication that still surprises me.

We are still the same rutting monsters we have always been. We haven't learned a thing about loving. We are still prehuman, which is nothing more than an animal with too much brains and not the wit to use them. We are still running from what we know we can be, deep down inside. We have never accepted our state. He kept dragging the animal along with us.

The seeming disparity between what we can be and the current state of affairs defeated us for millennia. It seemed too vast a difference. Somehow, I never got confused by all of the drills and frills and thrills. I always knew they were only distractions.

If someone goes too far over the edge, they are locked up or sent to a psychiatrist/psychologist. We say *they* are the problem.

We say *they* have a problem. Not humanity. We wipe our hands of it and totally ignore that humanity continues to crumble away into more bombast, pompousness, and willing destruction.

A race that rises above all has to learn to love itself in order to succeed. We have to *be* human, not *act* human. There is only one way. It is not magic. It is not willpower. It is all wrapped up in the physical act of expressing love that must be *shared* and *mutually fulfilling*. It finally creates love and eliminates the angst. Nature has had it waiting for us all along. All we had to do was come out from under the rock.

The Approaching Cliff and Pinnacle

The precipice on which we stand stuns me. We are on the verge of such a tremendous change. If the worst, most stupoured of us have their way, it will be wholesale destruction.

If a few people open their eyes, we can overcome all of the nonsense with which we have filled our prehuman existence.

If not, just wait for the wrecking ball to claim our existence.

We are on the verge of all of the nonsense being thrown into the fire along with the inequality, inequity, inadequacy, grandstanding, finger-pointing, blame-shifting, meaningless and deadly dissension, pompous declarations, dissemblance, and repression used to avoid the only question that matters. What is missing from love? Or; why is humanity such a mess?

All of it is thrown into the bin along with our prehuman existence in a virtual instant, once we learn to love; or we continue to witlessly approach the cliff, remaining unfulfilled.

Once again, I think, I have done all I can. (as I hyperventilate)

I always feel that what I explain might seem too flighty. It is not. But, let me try to take another tack at explaining. The question, in this case, is why haven't we already done this?

Men can learn to last long enough to make the act of coitus an act of love. Why in the world haven't they done so, yet? That is, maybe, the strongest evidence that something is wrong. That we never addressed the issue makes it clear that we have been in hiding from the dilemma. Comprehending the entire picture was quite a tremendous effort (that no one need repeat, again). Putting together the pieces of the resolution to the actual problem that men face was simplistic in comparison.

So, obviously, something was holding us back. It is truly a matter of a sentient race burying its head in the sand to avoid its conscious awareness. That is disastrous. In order to do so, a tremendous effort had to be expended to blind the race thoroughly. To the animal, it felt like a matter of survival. Without coitus, the race would not survive. Without loving coitus, the human, sentient race will not succeed.

From one perspective, it was a huge sacrifice to make. From a human point of view, it was the biggest disaster on record.

I feel like there are a million facts, a million different ways to explain the same thing. I've covered many in the eleven books already published (though, *counting this one*, you will only find eleven books - i took one off of the shelves as rather redundant. i feel pretty much the same about every book between *Millennium* and this one, other than *This and That*)

I skipped quite a few traces of evidence and perspectives because I would have felt I was letting loose my bitterness regarding my own gender's willingness to indulge itself and the stupour at the cost of our humanity. I am not a big fan.

I feel a strong need to clarify at this point (as i do so often). I am not talking about utopia. I am just talking about a sane existence. Finally, humans donning their humanity. Finally, humans no longer acting out the part of a human while remaining only an animal with too much brains and awareness.

We can change in an instant. Okay, call it a geological 'instant'. It will take less than three generations, once we get started, to complete the course of fulfilling our sentient state, stabilizing our emotions, and beginning to act with reason.

Something about which I continue to wonder, is just how tremendous our future as humans can be? I expect amazing developments. It amuses me that *this* is the 'singularity' that so many have been propounding. It is not genetics. It is not AI. It is not technological wonders. It is humanity.

We encountered something we could not face and learned procrastination, deception, and delusion in order to avoid facing the issue that disconcerted, discommoded, discomfited, and discombobulated all of our ancestors until this moment in time. We *learned* to remain animals with too much brains.

It is time to unlearn all of the nonsense that we have bought hook, line, and sinker and learn just how simple it is to love.

It is not enough to *act* human. We must *become* human.

Interrupted

Let me explain one of the problems I have with no dialogue on this subject with someone that is sympathetic with what I am saying. As I look at the note below, I feel like it should be up front (opening passage) for Human. Or, at least, some version thereof. But, how in the world would I be able to make that determination without a woman's insights? All I have gotten from everyone, so far, is pushback or dumbfounded silence. Dumbfounded silence is, by far, the overwhelming response.

There are just so many pertinent insights, but which ones will convince humanity that it can be so much more than an animal if men just learn to love? Love is a human trait that should be common to all of humanity. I hate using the word love because of all of the connotations that don't apply. What I am talking about is self-respect and self-confidence that validates one's existence. Love starts with self and moves on from there. Men, trapped in their animal state, do not have a clue about love and women's love is damaged by men.

As I look back on the last fifteen years, I have to shake my head. Guy, Interrupted. Who would have thought that I would figure out the riddle??!?! Not me! I have always been one to go with the flow (sorry, but, again, it is the right word). I lost that for fifteen years. I got caught up in the realization that I knew why humanity was such a mess and spent the last fifteen years wracking my brain earnestly. That's not really my style.

I can finally see it all clearly now. How it all came together to interrupt my flow of life. Chasing to put down on paper what I had wondrously uncovered. Right at the pinnacle of which, as I was nearly finished with *Sentience*, amazement in the form of a girl that is new under the sun, hit me broadside. Both were mysteries worth exploring. Between the two, each on the same order of amazement, I was caught   (ouuu, i like it)   for an additional eight years.

I was just idly plugging along studying the biggest puzzle of all: humanity. Not humans, but humanity. Think big picture. If you can. And, BAM!, I figured it out. It all fell in place in a single afternoon. Then, I tried to explain for the next fifteen years.

It's just weird. In every way, I honed my skills to do so. From my career, my penchant for honesty, my curiosity, the ease of life, and the profound effort to challenge myself, to my pursuit of love. Not intentionally. More haphazardly. I just knew what wouldn't work. I always thought of myself as a strategist when it came to my career. Well, let's just say I was inadvertently prepared by life for the quest, the quandary of humanity's insane state.

I have to say, "thank you, life" while gritting my teeth. Not exactly what I would have in mind for a entrancing life but, then again, without humanity becoming human there is no amazing life. There is only the unnecessary stress, misery, and madness.

Funny thing. I could not accept that my life could be just fine while so many suffer and the whole of humanity is vectored towards destruction. I guess, in all ways, one could say I just couldn't settle and, essentially, ignored everyone that did, more and more so over a lifetime (only one exception, so far).

There is human and there is not human. There is love and there is some shadow of love that is best labeled the mad, instinctual lust of an animal. Don't misinterpret. Lust is good but, for a human, it is not good until it is accompanied by love. It is the pursuit of love interrupted. That sentence may best encapsulate the problem that we face. Our intransigent, dumbfounded determination to remain no more than an animal has done us in, so far.

Anyways, I'm feeling pretty good at the moment. I know what I have accomplished, even if no one else does. In this life, there is only so much I can do without some help.

For one person, I must say excuse me. *Caught* between intruding and walking away, it was a torrent, a hurricane. The attraction remains phenomenal. Throw that into the mix with a seemingly nutty quest and what do you get?

I finally realized it wasn't explaining the problem that was driving me mad, it was understanding the problem that had me up against the wall.

I knew what the problem was for going on fifteen years but understanding the links and the breadth, the actual inner workings and extended consequences of the problem, was another matter entirely. It drove me to distraction.

Now I get it entirely and I'm anxious no longer. The explanations I am providing will just have to do. I'm not going to get all stressed about it. Words are not my forte but I've done what I can. Humanity will understand sooner or later. I laid it out well enough. After *Human*, I can't imagine a more thorough explanation. *A Sentient Perspective* and *Millennium* explain it well. The rest of the books are on target enough for anyone that is not drowning in the stupour of the animal.

Heck, if I get another lifetime I'll make it happen with love and dialogue. I just can't fret about it in this life any longer. There's no point. I hate to rely on another lifetime but there's not much else to do.

I can say with complete confidence that we aren't the mess we think we are. It is clear that we can end our madness (I was going to use the word 'craziness' but there is a good kind of crazy) and behave like full-fledged emotionally stable humans, instead of dumbfounded animals. The madness is not inherent. Nature provided that which can set us free from the bonds of stupour. All we need to do is utilize what Nature provided.

We howl to be free. Here is the freedom we've been looking for. Freedom from the stupour of the animal and the misery that is a direct result of the stupour. It's not inherent. It is renewed with each generation. It can be on its way out in one generation and be a distant memory in three.

Now that I've taken the stress (that i had avoided and studied when in the flow) out of my equation, I think I may be able to put the words in a clear, insightful version. We'll just have to see. Without dialogue, I remain concerned.

With each book, my rage would get jacked to the hilt. The massive scam that we have played on ourselves for the last three millennia is just mind boggling. And, yes, women were complicit in the coverup, though I still believe they had good reason. Think Sappho.

I began to sense the absence of fury (mostly) while writing *Human* (yeah, I'll get around to publishing it sooner or later. I guess I'm still looking for something that will make it complete, full circle).

Now that I think about it, I expect every human, as they launch into the future tense of split infinity, will feel the same outrage. Anyone that has spent more than prepuberty under the influence of the animal will feel that rage. I can't see any other way. It is the same rage that every youthful generation feels before they succumb to the dumbfounded state.

I'll say it again. That is what I sense in the woman that I adore. She shows the outrage better than anyone. She shows it from a woman's perspective, which should be rage and outrage. Surprisingly, most other women play the game the way it was dealt but not Her. She plays the game to her advantage and plays it so well. She is new under the sun. Probably not for that particular characteristic but for others that knock me back every time I consider them.

And there I go, full circle. It fueled me on that She felt the rage and outrage and put voice to it. I don't think She's ever understood that. I'm not sure She even understands her rage but, somehow, like me, she felt it at a visceral level. I'm not sure if She can't see past the rage to understand there is a resolution or She just revels in the rage and payback and doesn't worry about resolution.

Hmmm, how to describe. On the one hand, I had the revelation that we can be human. On the other I ran across a woman that is new under the sun. Really new under the sun.

How could I not become dizzy with wonder between the two?

You want wonder? As I tie the two wonders together, I get a most pronounced form of wonder (serendipity all over the place). It all begins to fit together like the pieces of the puzzle. I had always wanted a woman to want me for *all* of my qualities. I did not want it interrupted by any lack. Especially the most essential; the inspiration, the essence, for love. I guarantee you any man that desires a woman desires to make loving coitus. Most can't (about 90% to 99% of them). Anything less is a tremendous gaping hole in a loving agenda and I felt it deeply. Most become numbed to the paltry sum of love available in a world in which we remain a mad prehuman race.

Every man that I have talked to about it has defended his position of failure. The worst, of course, are those that won't even admit that there is need for anything more than rutting like an animal (orgasm for the woman is not even a consideration; "I am brute, hear me mumble pompously (sorry; there's that rage)) They still feel they have the 'right' to have sex with a woman (think the stupid, stupoured (might makes right) preposterous Incel and TRP). They are seriously messed up. They are closest to the animal. Look around at the obnoxious leaders in the press and you will see just such.

Those that find ways to compensate the woman in some form (I'm not sure that is always even orgasm) are partially human. They are the one thats always attempt to defend their position, which makes it clear that they think their position needs defending. They are right. It is surely better than nothing, but not as good as it should be. Women are treated as humans. That's good. The man is still not quite sure he is completely human. That's not so good. Why should men not learn to make loving coitus? Because our ancestors were all blinded to the possibility and inadvertently scuttled it for future generations?

There is no reason in the world for men to continue to rut like an animal. It is all just the bluff of an animal hiding their weakness (which is just insane) rather than the conscious thought of a human being to realize that he can love. He is not just an animal. A human being realizes that loving coitus is well within every man's reach.

Yes, men's compensatory efforts please the woman. But, does it please the man? The problem remains the man. Men will remain unsettled until they can make coitus a loving event. Because they can.

The answer I get is always the same, "well, she's okay with it." No doubt, but are you? There is never an answer to that. It is the hopelessness of desperation combined with the helplessness of being dumbstruck by the issue. It is disastrous to our humanity.

I was caught in the same trap and there was only one way out for me. I could not defend any other answer than loving coitus as an option. It is not necessary that loving coitus is consummated but it is critical that it is available. None of the many options that men excuse and defend, *in the absence of loving coitus*, in order to compensate made the slightest sense to me ... and, yet, I was flummoxed to find no answer for most of a lifetime. No one had taken a close look at the man's involvement in the failure of coitus. It is just quickly brushed under the rug *and accepted.* I finally read page after page of farcical web suggestions. That is when it dawned on me. Everyone was taking the man's limited span of time during coitus for granted.

It shouldn't have taken me a lifetime to figure that out. I excuse that easily. It has been scuttled to just such an extent and, no man had found the answer and made the effort to make it well known yet. It is the underlying impetus to avoid the question that finally hit home. Something was unnecessarily murky. I had to prove that a sentient human race (not this or that individual) has the wits to overcome and make loving coitus.

There is a quote from two thousand years ago that fits (i paraphrase): "the road to heaven is like threading the eye of a needle". I could not accept that, as a human being, I could not overcome what ails coitus. The eye of the needle has always been wide open for *human* men. It has been made murky and seemingly impossible only by the animal legacy. All we had to do was get out from under the brambles.

It took me most of my life to come to that conclusion and I left a lot of wreckage behind because of the sexual drive that overrides reason. That is, reason is overcome when a man fails. This is the outrage that drove me up the wall. Why did humanity accept that men cannot consistently make coitus a loving event?

It's just ridiculous, if you think about it. But, it also makes sense. All of our thoughts regarding the act of coitus are interrupted during the act, especially in men. How can they contemplate seriously what they are doing if their thoughts are interrupted during coitus. I know of only one man that had what it took to think about coitus dispassionately after the act. I think he figured out how to make it work. Though I can't attest to it, everything about his life points to it. It was another one of those strange encounters of my life. He was willing to try to explain how he became a successful lover but no one was willing to listen.

Women seem to have never dared ask the question openly and, even if they did, it got shot down by men, never published, never even mentioned. Sappho comes to mind, again. She may be the only woman in all of history that got the word out to some extent.

Things change, though. That is what sentience and Nature are all about. We learn and we progress. So far, rutting coitus is a gaping hole in our progress. We have denied ourselves the most important way in which we become human. *For no good reason!*

This is where it all came together for me. One explanation, at least, for which I have been looking. In the absence of loving coitus, a man feels like he is selling damaged goods. Not too bad if they are willing to perform cunnilingus or something but, still, not the whole package. The man remains reduced.

Now, as I realize that any man can perform loving coitus, I am a complete package. There is no more hesitation in my manner. Only certainty. If I find a woman to love me, I am the whole package. Men, that have been held back since the caves, are no longer on clearance sale.

This is another interesting aspect of our prehuman state. Men are so desperate to find any way in which to get laid (while realizing they are horrible at the act) that no real relationships could develop. There is always the overhang of the failure. Even the best of relationships begin to crumble as the man realizes what is going on and loses confidence and respect for himself.

Do you see? This has been so hard to explain and I feel it is what is missing from the understanding of others as to the devastating consequences of the failure of humanity to make coitus a loving event. "It's complicated" was written for this very use. Going from animal to prehuman to human is complicated.

Sometimes I wonder if the question on everyone's mind isn't, "how are you going to get *all* men to learn to love?" If so, it is the wrong question. The right question is,"how does humanity learn to love?" And, "how difficult is it for a man to learn how to love physically?" (answer: dead easy, once we get over the dumbfounded confusion) accompanied by the realization that men are not just animals (though many think of themselves as only animals). They can think. They have just avoided doing so for three millennia due to fear of exposing their failure (that 'exposure' is another hilarious instance of our dumbfounded state; it's confirmed every time a man fails! do you get how ridiculous the situation is now??).

Getting all men to provide orgasm for a woman in some form (other than coitus) would be like herding cats.

Getting all men to learn loving coitus is just a matter of getting through three millennia of the dumbfounded defeatism and surrender. Once that is done. Once men can realize that they can love as they desire, they will all desire to become human.

You don't have to convince a man that he needs to learn to love physically. It all falls in place when he realizes he is human and, thereby, privileged to have the wherewithal to love a woman physically the way for which Nature provided (coitus). Anything less would always be a battle. That battle is not human. It is only prehuman antics.

Until men learn this essential fact about their humanity, they are not yet human. If men knew for certain that it was possible for any man to learn to love, that it is as natural for a human male to make love as it is to breathe, then no man would pass up the chance. They would be lining up in droves to learn how to love. Especially the young that haven't been inundated with the misery, stupour, and defeatism of the older generations.

It has to become just like talking. It has to become an expectation of a human male that they know how to love.

Women already know, though their loving has been blunted all along.

Do you see? We just need to have enough men proclaim that they have learned how to make love and have logged enough time as a human being to realize just how easy it is to do - *for a human*. Then, our emotional stability will begin to kick in for the *human race*, not a few individuals (and, believe me, today it is very few individual men that are emotionally stable and not dysfunctional and disoriented by their human state of failure).

And, oh, by the way, *none* of this is going in *Human* unless I get some feedback that it helps someone understand. If everyone remains dumbfounded, so be it. I'll just hope I get the chance of another lifetime to do it all from scratch.

Interruption

As I delve further, I find another way to put it. You have to understand that I have had all of these concepts ratting around in my head for ages. This one idea, validation, has been hanging around forever. It's just a matter of fitting them together in such a way that they make sense.

In Interrupted, I begin to get into the broader aspects of love.

Today, there are a jillion reactions to love and love's interruption. One the most common is the feeling of betrayal or the feeling of unworthiness. Both reactions usually come with a big dose of devastation, as if one's world has been turned upside down. There are reasons built into our prehuman condition that force those feelings of unworthiness and/or betrayal. It is a story we've made up that makes no sense in the real, sentient world. It's all about self-validation. (i know someone that would laugh the asses off to hear me say that).

Honestly, listening to love songs over the span of life of a lyricist is fascinating.   You can almost see the ongoing devastation take effect, as attempt after attempt to love gets crushed. It's no different for anyone else. It's just that lyricists put it down in words. You can see that they finally settle for less - like damn near everyone.

Love should be an unmitigated celebration. That   doesn't mean that its end means one should feel devastated. Disappointment, sure, but not devastation. I go back and forth on whether love will become a lifelong experience or not, once we become human. Honestly? I can make an argument either way.

This is the strongest argument I have developed for love lasting a lifetime. If the impediments are as facile as they seem, then the idea of sharing one's life fully with another is a powerful incentive. It's important. Too bad it's so broken. Everyone learns to settle, one way or another.

This is where validation comes into he picture. Why is it that we feel invalidated when someone doesn't love us back or changes their mind or screws with us? That's on them. It is the lack of self-validation.

I've explained in detail why men don't feel valid in their existence. Because of that, they pick apart the validity of the woman. One might say that is the source of misogyny that places it on the shoulders of every man. It goes back at least three millennia.

Settling never sat well with me, so what else was there to do? I never lost my feeling of validity, but there was certainly a problem that I was not facing. It became clear that there was a problem and it was much bigger than just me. Somewhere along the line I realized it was the male gender that had a problem.

Kinda obvious, really, but they throw such tantrums when they don't get their way or they feel threatened. The loving Rite of Passage is all that the male gender needs to learn.

Why is it so hard for anyone else to see the instability built into the system the way it is built today. A little initial effort on the part of the man that will end up being no effort at all can change the world - because he is a thinking human being, not just an animal. He can learn to love. Not trained into it by rote but immersed in it - like a human being. It's all up to the male gender.

Think of it this way, maybe. Those original men, thousands of years ago, were pretty new at thinking and they weren't very good at it. Now, throw in the mind-boggling experience of orgasm that one wants to repeat and often and the bothersome reality that the woman is getting nothing at all. How would one expect a barely cogent human male to deal with that? Those early ancestors couldn't think their way out of a wet paper bag, much less the physical aspect of the mind-boggling experience of orgasm and failure to make it mutual.

All that is necessary is to think one's way *through* the experience rather than just focus on the ultimate experience for oneself. It is an entirely new effort to overcome the reactionary, instinctual response of the animal. It never even crossed our mind that a man (not an animal) can last as long as he desires *because* he is not just an animal. He can think his way through in order to make it the most incredible loving experience.

Do you see how even other alternatives to loving coitus don't validate, *on their own*, the feeling of failure? The failure that bothers men isn't really the failure to pleasure woman. It is the failure to make the most natural form of sex human. We've known all along that we should be able to do better but the confounding stories and lies we have told ourselves all along have abrogated the possibility.

It undermines a man's humanity to realize he cannot. He is at a loss. His humanity is invalidated, it seems. Of course, he wants to invalidate everyone else. Other men might not be invalid. That makes him suspicious. Women will, sooner or later, learn that he is invalid. That makes him downright paranoid.

The best a man can do, today, other than stumble upon some way in which to last a few minutes is to humble himself. It is an unnecessary humility. Humanity isn't built for humility as a way of life.

It's, of course, way more complicated than that. The man is attracted to women (duh.). So, he does everything he can to attract a woman. Then, once he has her, he tries to figure out what is wrong with her. Why would she accept someone that is so lousy at sex?

Do you see? We have had no choice but to accept alternatives to loving coitus in order to make the experience mutual. It is a gaping hole in our wholeness. I repeat that the alternatives are not the problem to calm those that feel a need to justify the alternatives. It is the absence of loving coitus that causes all the problems. Not the presence of alternatives.

One storyline imprinted itself on my mind. George from Seinfeld (it might have been a movie) played it out. It was over the top, of course, but it really burned the idea into my head because it was so ridiculous.   George was attracted to a stunningly beautiful woman that seemed interested in George, so he became hung up about a woman's toes (big toe?) that was shaped funny in order to justify blowing her off.   That is the most extreme way of doing it.   Blow someone off *before* you get caught.

It's a double or triple whammy.   First, the story we tell ourselves is that we are invalid until we fall in love.   Parents also often pick apart children to assure that one has no confidence in oneself.   They consider it part of their job to crush confidence.

(I really don't want to get into why that is directly related.   You should be able to get there on your own.)

Then, a loving relationship is broken apart by the reason that seldom, if ever, is mentioned.   (which is what all of the books are about)   The understanding of the two genders are so tangential to each other that they never intersect.   The man wallows in his ineffectiveness and the woman can't even see it. Of course, the man does his best to act like everything is alright on that front (just one of the many false fronts he learns in order to hide his failure).   It's not that men are from Mars and women from Venus.

I guess another good point is that this all makes one begin to wonder if any intimate relationship ever fails for some other valid reason?   I couldn't say.   I don't think a valid reason has ever been suggested.   You may think that some other condition can be traced as the source of problems.   I say that we cannot tell until the lack of loving coitus is eliminated.   Finances is the usual scapegoat today.   That is so specious as to cause a blinding glare.

In general, as far as any and all of the problems of humanity (the ones that humanity causes) are invalid until loving coitus is an alternative.

Love and self-love is part of human life.   It is not part of prehuman life.   A person should grow into their lives loving themselves and never find it invalidated ever.   If they find someone to love, that is spectacular and probably the common case.   It may even last a lifetime - for a human.

It is a huge step that men are finally beginning to realize it is virtually none of them that perform loving coitus.   The next step, of course, is that they learn that they can. They are human. It's not even difficult once we get past of the fear of failure, exposure, and shame that the animal instilled into the stupour.

These two posts belong as the opening passage of *Human*, but no way. I'll probably bury it in Bits & Pieces. It'll take more thought than I am willing to invest to clean it up on my own.

The one that really drives me nuts is that I know I portray it all very black and white and I pick apart the guys' responsibility for the mess with more emphasis than I should. Of course, women are messed up also (especially this self-validation thing), but just keep in mind that, if it weren't for men shunning their responsibility so long ago that it doesn't even show up, there would be no such problems. The questioning it caused among women is maybe even worse than the more blatant misogyny.

Maybe think of it as the witless state of the animal being exacerbated by the failure of men combined with the knowledge that it damn well makes no sense for men to fail at loving coitus.

Sanity

I have had almost no presence of mind. Today, everyone must make a choice. Either presence of mind or sanity.

Once we become human there will be no choice to be made. Everyone will be able to be present and sane.

I've often wondered why it has to all be so painful. This is the reason. We are in shatters because we either accept prehumanity's awful conditions and keep our presence or we keep our sanity.

I took it to the limit. Truly. In every way. I lost all presence by stepping away and inspecting our mess like a bug under a glass. Now, if it catches on, we can be present and sane.

I am now very present. I don't particularly like it at my age and all on my own and no one with whom to share. That's the breaks, aye?

Leverage

Since this is the fulcrum by which we attain our sentience and sanity, I just want to make sure it is clear.

I am certain anyone that is paying attention must admit that the human race, if it were viewed as a single individual, is insane.

I am not suggesting utopia, I am just suggesting sanity.

Men's self-confidence and self-respect is undermined nearly daily after achieving puberty by constant realization that they fail to perform the act of love in the way that it is crystal clear it should operate for a sentient race. It drives many mad. From some views, I should take the 'y' out of the previous sentence.

We are not an animal. Our heightened awareness makes it clear that there should be more to coitus. It is foolish to believe that a sentient male cannot overcome the limitations placed on the male animal. Women should consistently gain the same pleasure as the man. As our heightened awareness has sharpened over time, so has this conundrum. It makes us uncomfortable. As we continue to avoid the issue, the tumult increases.

We are, essentially, avoiding our fulfillment and emergence into our sentient state by continuing to look away. Many will have a difficult time accepting this premise. I hope I have explained it well enough. I can't imagine how to explain better without reincarnating.

Even more so, is the shock of finally realizing our full emergence into a sentient state by learning to love is exactly what Nature has provided and *intended* for a sentient race all along! Nature left it to us to succeed ... or not.

Our awareness has been a subtle thing that has remained roaming around in our subconscious breaking all the furniture. It has been cursed down through the ages. In the West, since the myth of The Garden of Eden was conceived, the desire was to put an end to sentience. "Dumb as a rock is a state of bliss," if I were to try to put it into words. It could never work.

I see a lot of correlations between the deluded state of the West and the fascist tendencies. Both are dumb as a rock.

It confounds a person to realize the transcendent experience that men have always been given by the female cannot be returned in kind. It boggles a young man's mind (and probably a woman's, at least one that knows she can feel the same transcendence). It has debilitated every generation. The boldest finally began to find some other way. Kudos, but not enough. Our sentience can and, therefore, must do better.

Men keep trying to fight perceiving a sentient reality because it is like looking into an abyss. It disrupts their minds.

My estimates of 99% failure rate are based on **_unassisted_** coitus lasting long enough to fully pleasure the woman (which is the point), which seems to run somewhere between 10 to 15 minutes. Any other definition is meaningless. Two or three minutes, for instance, as success? Success of what?

I'm sure the most intransigent beasts among us will say that's impossible. It is impossible. For an animal.

Once men realize that they have been fooling themselves for millennia, they will realize how easy it is for a sentient human being *because they can think*. They can direct their muscles and overcome the animal's instincts. This will be especially easy for those young folks just emerging into pubescence, as they get it right from the start and don't learned all of the wrong lessons.

Do you see the double-edged sword here? How the issue forced humanity to limit its thinking faculties? How we had to shut down thinking to a great extent to avoid thinking about the issue that seemed disastrous to contemplate at all?

Can you conceive what it means that half of the human race has beaten itself down in defeat at the hands of the act of coitus because they never took into account that they can think?

The ramifications are vast and mind-boggling.

Can you conceive what it will mean when all men walk with their heads held high, their self-respect and confidence completely in tact? Not some false facade to get through the day.

I have tried to study this deeply. I have attempted to discover something else that could undermine a fully developed human's natural state of stable emotions, sentience, reason, and love.

I cannot find a single other instance that could undermine the human state of sentience like the very common, persistent, relentlessly repetitive failure of the act of love in its most pristine, physical form of coitus.

The alternative of believing we are less is just ridiculous.

This is key. We have never really considered our sentient state's final fulfillment. We have always gone along with the idea that we are no more than an animal with too much brains. We have believed that the sentient state is fully developed. That is not the case. A few men must step forward and learn to love.

Alternatives of "Me"

As I said in a previous section, kudos to those that find some other way to assure the woman achieves pleasure.   I would expect that most keep some reasonable shred of their self-respect by doing so. It begins to bypass the thought, "it's all about me"

But, can any human male say that they are comfortable that they cannot make loving coitus? First, it is necessary to get past the belief that there is nothing to be done. That is the only reason that I can surmise that so many heartily defend their position.

We are sentient, for goodness' sake! It is utter failure of our sentient state to say we can do no better.   Our love remains compromised when we are *forced* to do it some other way.

We have been so programmed to expect failure for so long that we just never even really study the problem. We just accept it. That makes us an animal, for all intents and purposes.   Look closely at the studies.   They all say it is a 'mystery' and are content to leave it at that. They ask no questions and measure time intervals. They specify the various stages of ejaculation but that's it! They never even query seriously why the time limit?

Even worse, there are some paradigms about the failure and how to 'improve' that are globally accepted and utterly wrong. That tells you how far back in time the nonsense was concocted. It has never changed. Since before the *Kama Sutra*.

The point is, humans can do better than animals. If we hadn't been scared out of our wits long ago, we could have figured out just how easy it is to improve some time ago. All of the male gender would have put an effort into it rather than one guy.

It is the defining difference between animal and human.

It wasn't easy to figure out the fundamental issues. But, the only *real* barrier was overcoming the delusions, conditioning, and paradigms that have been pounded into our brains since birth.   The worst is the programmed response to avoid the subject. "At all costs, don't look too closely! Don't spend much time thinking about your utter failure!" That is maniacal instinct drilled so deeply we accepted it for three millennia.

It is not an option to continue to be lousy at coitus. Loving coitus is human. It is a human imperative that we have ignored.

The layers of obstruction to thought starts with sex and, then, finally, hidden deeply, the trembling question of what is wrong with coitus, which correlates directly with what is wrong with humanity. Our feeble attempts at love are depressing. We make excuses for love. Hidden below it all is the ridiculous belief in a time limit that is the end result of animal instincts that a human can easily overcome with the slightest effort, once realized.

Do you see now why we continue to approach the cliff? In our efforts to avoid the subject of sex we have also been avoiding the subject of what is wrong with humanity. We have just accepted that humanity is broken beyond repair. Most would rather run off that cliff than face the real issue.

I will add my usual disclaimer to this one, since I feel I have to put it somewhere, otherwise people get all bent out of shape:

This does not mean that every man and woman wants coitus. There are many other options; but coitus should *not* be excluded from the because it fails! Its exclusion causes all of the problems of humanity because it is inhuman that it remains a failure.

The highly intelligent and exceedingly aware sentient race of humanity must be certain that it has overcome the debilitating feature of animal sex that makes coitus less desirable for a human, sentient creature that expects to fulfill its loving desires. Make no mistake, that goes for both genders.

The only reason men don't seem to care is because they are certain they have failed and that there is nothing they can do about it, so no reason to talk about it. "Grin and bear it" in spades! They want to avoid the subject like the plague. I hope I have explained well enough why this is so debilitating for men.

The saying goes that men want sex and woman want love. Far from it. Men have just accepted their defeat and women accepted their loss. Can you see now how that grinds away at the mental state? Of course all sentient creatures of either gender want to love and be loved! The circle must be completed!

I guess another way to look at it is that we prove (validate?) our sentient state by overcoming the debility of animal coitus.

The craziest little amusing scene jumped into my head as I reread the previous paragraphs. I can see Nature standing with a stamp of approval. "Okay, humanity's sentience has now been established and validated!" STAMP! "Next!"

The Arduous Journey, Part II

When I was studying cultures, institutions, and religions, history, anthropology, philosophy, sociology, psychiatry, and psychology this is what turned me off. We never ever look at the race as a whole. *Never!* While there are some interesting studies that trigger interesting clues, in all we remain convinced that the quirks are individual and not induced by a species-wide dilemma. Again, it looks like inadvertent, and yet, purposeful misdirection. Especially since men set all of the stage.

While the quirks show up in great abundance in some individuals, it is a species-wide phenomenon. The individuals of which you are probably thinking right now, are not even the worst ones. The ones that matter. Another set of blinders.

It all adds up to nice words that don't mean a thing (well, in some cases there is value; in most cases, it becomes an awful, irrational deception regarding humanity's insanity; often placing the blame well wide of its mark). It stuns me, in retrospect, that we never caught on to the fact that there is something fundamentally wrong with our current state of existence.

What really shows the state of the deception is that *everyone* is pointing their finger at someone else. *They* are to blame. Not *you!* The accepted fact is that sentience is a failure rather than something is missing. We don't place the blame accurately. This stems from the width, depth, and breadth of the taboo/stupour.

Any words trying to interpret this human sentient existence until we accept that we are human, sentient and continue to fail are gibberish. It's just embarrassing. We have run around *acting* like we are human because we know damn well what it should be like (self-respect; confidence in oneself, esteem, one's own humanity as well as the race's; dignity, honour, integrity, compassion, empathy, and love, etc.

Can you see how we try to mimic these characteristics? The false bravado, pompous proclamations, etc. It's all an act.

It is a far cry from *being* human. The facade of *acting* human breaks down on a whim, at the drop of a hat. It all falls apart regularly and thoroughly, as it seems to be breaking down at this moment on a major scale, as so often happens. We are in a horrific turmoil as the animal, once again, attempts to steer the ship for a collision course with the rocky shore. We need to get off of the stage of theater of the Absurd in a hurry.

The thought of existentialism (or deconstructionism: same thing, different decade, different word, far more acidic content) as an answer rather than just another bluff, scam, and misdirection when not enraging me, makes me want to puke. It is pure defeatism, just as is our surrender to the failure of loving coitus. (a lot of hyperventilating going on)

We spew out words blindly because something has always been missing. We are just making stuff up until we grasp our sentience and our sentient state.   Sentience is not a failure. Sentient reality is not up for discussion and misdirection. Humanity is a failure because it has not yet grasped its sentience. Humanity has not yet accepted Nature's fulfilling gifts.

Another phrase that has grated all my life is 'perception is reality'. That underlines the animal's perspective. It is witless pontification that has no sentient meaning. Perceptions that don't match reality are called delusions: blatant, conscious or unconscious deceits. We are in the midst of such an incredible instance of that stupour right now. It is appalling. It is a matter of the dumbed down animal sensing a vast change that it fears.

I can still remember exactly where I was standing when the realization of what went wrong for humanity hit me like a supernova. All of it, all of the quirky behaviours of humanity fell in place as the stunning realization hit me that being lousy at coitus was *not just me*. It is not an occasional failure. It is a failure that can only be measured on the scale of humanity. A failure that finally made all of the weird behaviour of man make sense in a nonsensical way. Failure is standard procedure and no one wants to talk about it.

Yes, the best of men have found ways to fill the gap. They are still few and far between. It leaves a lot of men and relationships hanging and never really confirms our sentient state. It leaves whole cultures (my guess the majority of the world population) still banning any thought about sex in any form and certifying and justifying treating women like slaves, objects for the men's sexual pleasure. All because the man cannot admit his failure.

Do you begin to see how it adds up. *Men's* sexual pleasure. It is difficult for me to explain how this comes about. It is why I stress the phrase, men take, women give, and it all starts in bed. We are still children when we first experience puberty and sex. In the cauldron of the sexual experience, men *learn to take*. It's all they can do. It gets burned into the psyche.

I'm getting wound up, once again ... Another that drives me crazy is legislation to ameliorate all of our ills. The perfect example, as always, is misogyny, domestic violence, rape, and the whole plethora of issues regarding the demented human mindset when it comes to sex. I mean, I don't blame women for howling about it all and asking for something, anything to be done. What else could they could do?

But, really, that doesn't change a thing. It doesn't make us more sentient. It doesn't resolve our demented state. It just puts a lid on the pressure cooker that always ends up exploding.

Addressing it with legislation has been the only alternative but it only blinded us further. For all of that, it also just doesn't work. It can never really resolve the issue. It hardly has an impact on the violent nature of the prehuman when it involves the sexual tension between two genders. The matter essentially remains unaddressed. It does, though, highlight the problems. It also highlights the behaviour as inhuman. I often described it as the armed camps of the two genders.

(hyperventilation done)

There is so much wrong with legislating our existence, it is difficult to know where to start. It is a ludicrous animal's effort to deal with human problems. It just delays the inevitable. What we are admitting is that we can't *act* human with any sincerity. The prehuman will always find a way around the laws, like rats in the wainscoting. We are seeing it happen today.

It is not a rational, stable, balanced way to live. It is not sentient. It is the animal contending with its sentient nature in a poor and fumbling manner.

Disparity

I have tried to explain in many of the books the difference between our current state in which we attempt to force the prehuman to *act* human and the state in which a sentient being *becomes* human because it is sane.　The race must become *internally* driven to *be* human before we can ever succeed at donning the mantle of sentience.　In other words, we have to remove the one instance in life that takes away our humanity.

Right now, we *act* out a part.　Outside forces (e.g. legislation, cultural peer pressure, religious mores, intellectual morals, corporate inducements to act like an animal) attempt to convince a prehuman *act* to in a certain way.　In most cases, it is a desire to force people to *be* nice, have respect for oneself, act nobly. The prehuman will only play out the part as long as the wind blows favorably.　There is no conviction at all.

A human, with its sentience in tact, will not revert.

Misogyny is a fine example.　It doesn't make sense in any context, once you look closely.　It is the bewildered animal taking out its frustration on the more sentient gender for its own failure.　The debasement of the female gender is going nowhere until we become human.

A male gender that is confident in itself (i.e. sentient and loving) would never even consider it.

Why would the male gender maintain a system that grates on existence and the relationship between the two genders?　Women will tell you, misogyny is encountered every day in micro-aggressions and, often, in macro-aggressions.

Why would men want to drive women mad and/or away? Men want sex, so why the undercurrent of mistreatment?

Wouldn't it make more sense to treat women like men were seeking heaven (much closer to the truth)?　They certainly want to have sex with women.　Isn't it insane to drive them away?　Do you see the disparity?

It may not be obvious to you yet, but misogyny exists because men are lousy at coitus.　It is one of those pieces of the puzzle that makes no sense otherwise.　Men's comprehensive failure bothers them so much that they take it out on women.　They know it's not right. They can't help themselves. In fact, those that go far down that road clearly hate themselves.

INCEL and TRP are perfect examples. They whine that women don't want to sleep with them. This clearly indicates they know exactly what the problem is. Their model was invented long ago. It echoes The Garden of Eden. The Red Pill (TRP) really cracks me up. TRP connotes a desire to overcome delusion. It is *hilarious* that they chose that label. They are drowning in delusions. (okay, the hyperventilation continues)

We rid ourselves of the animal's problem, which is failed coitus, by realizing we are human and can easily overcome the broken animal's rendition of coitus and simultaneously overcome the very prehuman problem of the two gender's armed camps as well as the many, many demented offshoots of other less directly related ills caused by all of the delusions.

The *internally* generated basis for being human will not fail and will have no desire to rationalize beastly behaviour because there will be no beastly behaviour.

I expect emotional stability, rational thought, and a loving perspective to resolve most issues in two or three generations.

While I am certain we will have attained our sentient state in full within three generations (maybe sooner), I am not certain we will have undone all of the issues we have created in the preceding three millennia in that timeframe.

There is another factor to keep in mind, though that will accelerate eliminating the dystopia. The liberation of 90% of our brain from the dysfunctional uses of avoiding the issue to which it is applied today will help move us forward rapidly. Liberation from the stupour will free up a lot of brain power for more estimable efforts. I find that encouraging.

Endings

The most annoying aspect of this whole effort is seeing how the prehuman clings to its despair like a shield against their own humanity and potential for love. It has been quite trying.

It is a good thing that I am more resilient than the stupour.

Truly anonymous

All I really want is for my work, these words, to finally succeed at transforming humanity into something truly human. Whickwithy is a pretty obvious pseudonym. I would like to keep it that way.

Sigh. Besides there being so little to discover about me, I would just as soon no one tried. After essentially isolating for fifteen years, no one really knows me.

What do you need to know about me? I love women right down to my bones. Women, in general, and one in particular, have been my guiding light. They display the humanity that the male gender must learn to achieve through loving coitus.

The one that I adore I am pretty certain is mystified by my adoration. That breaks my heart in so many ways and, yet, it makes sense, also. That pretty much sums up my life.

Other than that? *Until* we fulfill our humanity, I'll agree with the statement, "Life sucks and, then, you die." and, yet, never utter the phrase because it is not human. It is only the despair that has continued to filter down through our prehuman state.

It is not the end state of sentience, but it can be the end state for the human race if we do not wake up to our humanity.

"Life sucks and, then, you die; until we become human."

If you read my rhoetry, you will see why it kept me afloat. I was adamant, throughout my writing of rhoetry, that I would not end a rhoem on a sour note (there were only two exceptions when i was just that down-hearted). In other words, I might describe some monstrous condition in a rhoem, point out a despair that the prehuman endures but, always, I would end on a positive note. "Daunting Realms" and one of my favorites, "The Travelers" are very good examples of what I mean.

Funny thing. It wasn't like I made a conscious effort to work the rhoems that way. Not until much later in life. I didn't even really think about it until not too long ago.

Oh, yes, I always saw the monster and have always been convinced it was an illusion that could be brushed away like a puff of smoke (stated in my way more metaphorical poetic way of describing things). You have no idea how good it feels to finally prove (at least to myself) that I was right all along.

It's funny that what nearly broke me was not that. Oh no, only the dumb-founded silence of the masses as I revealed their humanity to them could do that - through eleven books.

If you leave me alone *and* I see humanity begin to take this seriously (and I don't die), I might continue to write. If you don't, I assure you whickwithy will become a ghost.

Trending

One last piece of evidence as well as a very suspicious absence in our sentient thought. As far as I know, we are the only animal on the planet that has no 'season' for sex. No, I'm not going to check to verify that is true. In the whole branch of animals, I guess it is possible and I just haven't heard about it (though, as I said, I scan a *lot* of information).

Anyways, the point is, why isn't this unusual characteristic of the human race ever mentioned when speaking of why we are so unusual? It seems to me to be another piece of evidence of how little we want to think about sex. Just do it. Gag. It should be just do it right. We are sentient.

And, one more concern about why no one seems to be able to break the barrier to our sentience. Is there some even deeper taboo that tells people, "Don't mess with sex! It's dangerous!" If so, just realize that is from the same nonsense that blocks any rational thought on LGBTQ in some circles.

One last word. If you have questions, read more of my books. There is no way I could cover everything in one book, though I have tried to pack this one with a lot of information. While I am sure I have not addressed every speck, I addressed *a lot!*

I won't be surprised at all if there are some typing errors in this book, though they really should be minimal. I've done this all on my own with zero help. I have really appreciated the need for an editor for a long time. Not a single person stepped up to help.

Whickwithy

whickwithy@gmail.com
Thank you for reading this book

I just thought it would be nice to reiterate the reason I use this photo. Considering I have spent the last fifteen years attempting to form my knowledge and awareness into something that can convey all of the nonsense that we have endured and how we finally eliminate it and become human, there has been a whole lot of snarling. The forty years before that, while I was just wondering what is wrong with the human race, it wasn't so bad. I used a shy lion at that point.

I hope the tone of this book changed radically from previous books. As I mentioned I was outraged, most of all, that it had to come down to me to explain (i am terrible at explaining, for hone thing). Also, I was outraged that it took us three millennia before anyone woke up to the fact that we are not yet sentient.

As I have tried to explain clearly, in retrospect, that is not a big surprise. I am now uncertain whether an earlier date would have worked as well for a variety of reasons. I will not be surprised if this book never makes the cut. As I said, I am terrible at explaining, *especially* when I can find no one with whom to share.